Sister Saint-Pierre & the Work of Reparation

A Brief History

REV. JANVIER

True Image of the Holy Face of our Lord Jesus Christ,
Religiously venerated and kept in Rome,
in the Basilica of Saint Peter, in the Vatican.

I mprimatur:

JOHN CARDINAL McCLOSKEY,

April 12, 1885.

Archbishop of New York.

Imprimatur:

CAROLUS,

Archiep. Turon,

16 Aprilis, 1882.

Malmouche, V. C.
May 8, 1884.

Preface

THE following work is a translation of the brief *Life of Sister Saint-Pierre* which was published by the Rev. Father Janvier at Tours in 1882 with the approbation of his archbishop. Her own account of her experiences, and remarkable manifestations of the divine favor, has been already given to the public by the instrumentality of the Carmelite Kuns of New Orleans. This *Life,* collated and completed by means of her letters and the annals of her monastery, was published by the Rev. P. Janvier, Dean of the Metropolitan Church of Tours and Director of the Priests of the Holy Face. It bears the imprimatur of the Archbishop of Tours; and the English translation is approved by the Archbishops of Baltimore and New Orleans, and by other prelates.

The present work by the devoted Father Janvier is, as he explains in his preface, an attempt to give the principal facts in the life of the saintly Carmelite, with an account of the Work of Reparation to which the Confraternity of the Holy Face is consecrated. We think it will be read by pious Catholics with much edification and profit. His Grace of Baltimore tells us that "her *Life* is calculated to promote piety and edification not only in cloistered institutions, but also in the ranks of the secular life."

The Archbishop of New Orleans warmly approves and recommends it, and declares "that he will be glad to see it rapidly diffused among the faithful, who will find it a treasure of edification and instruction calculated to inspire them with devotion to the Holy Face." The question of the virtues of Sister Saint-Pierre has not been raised at Rome, and the Holy See has thus far decided nothing in regard to the supernatural character of the revelations which she received. But, with the approbation of the Supreme Pontiff, the Confraternity of the Holy Face has been established, and there can be no reason to doubt the many miracles wrought through the instrumentality of M. Dupont, the Holy Man of Tours. The Confraternity of the Holy Face was established at St. Dizier in 1847, and at Tours in 1876, where now there is an association of priests especially devoted to its interests. It has been enriched by indulgences granted by Pius IX of blessed memory, and Leo XIII gloriously reigning.

The brief of Leo XIII dated December 9, 1884, recognizes the confraternity at Tours as legitimately established, and, "in order that it may daily increase, opens the treasures of the Church to its members who shall perform the devotions recommended by the rule." These indulgences are also applicable to the souls in Purgatory. Indulgences, both plenary and partial, had been accorded by His Holiness Pius IX in 1847, 1848, and 1876.

With this high sanction the confraternity has been erected in the United States.

This work, which now we recommend to the devout lovers of Jesus Christ, will fully, though briefly, explain the end of the devotion to the Holy Face of our Lord. By exciting in our souls a stronger personal love to our Redeemer it will lead us to a life more in union with Him. His blessed Face, which represents to us not only all the sorrows which He endured for our salvation, but also all the sweetness of His Sacred Heart, will be before us to attract us more powerfully day by day. It will wean us from sin, from the love of the world, and even from our own foolish pride. Then, with true loyalty, we will be able to make reparation to Him by deeds and words which love prompts and sanctifies. If there be a blessed work on earth, it is that of reparation. If there be an affection which can have complete power over the heart and intelligence, it is the love of our dearest Lord and Savior. We are convinced that the devotion to the Holy Face will be the means of sanctifying many souls, and that it is especially suitable to the needs of our day. The great Master and Teacher of holiness will accomplish much in us, if we will only seek to live in His sight and obey the motions of His grace. May He, of His infinite mercy, deign to show us the light of His countenance, and to look with love and blessing upon our feeble efforts to extend His reign in the hearts of men!

T. S. P.

New York, April 12, 1885.

Author's Preface

THIS little book has long been earnestly desired. Friends of the Carmelites and the *Life of Sister Saint-Pierre,* written by herself, have asked an abridgment of it which should be the counterpart of our notice on M. Dupont and the Work of the Holy Face. In responding to this desire, we have neglected nothing which could render this pious history interesting and popular, and at the same time make it serve as a means of propagating the Holy Work of Reparation. In this we believe we are obeying the orders of our Lord transmitted to his servant. "The Lord," says she, "asks of France a Work of Reparation which will be for her the *rainbow of mercy.* Ah! if it were extended to all the dioceses, all the cities, I would be without uneasiness, for God is faithful to his. promises. ... I have always said, and I still repeat it: *it is this which is to disarm the justice of God and save France.* Happy if they know how to profit by this means of salvation!"

A pious and eloquent layman recently said: "The social edifice is falling into ruins. Humanly speaking, nothing can sustain it. Perhaps you rely on God? On God!—as individuals, granted; but as a nation? Has not France driven him from her government, her laws, her morals? On God! when everywhere his Name is blasphemed ? On God! when his day is profaned and his Church attacked? All that is happening to us, is it not the expression of his just anger? Is it not precisely this anger that is first to be appeased? In truth, this accomplished, salvation becomes possible; *'for if God is for us who shall be against us?'* Now, the sure means of softening his anger, and consequently the great means of salvation—the one which God himself, before reducing us to extremities, has deigned to recommend—is Reparation."[1]

O you who love the Church and France, read, and from the teachings of the pious Carmelite of Tours learn in what consists of this Reparation, and, in acting upon it, what you have to do.

P. Janvier.

Festival of the Finding of the Holy Cross, May 3, 1882.

---

1. Allocution of General Foloppe, November 12, 1881.

Contents

Chapter 1

HER YOUTH

I t is to Catholic Brittany, strong in faith and great in heroic virtues,
that we are indebted for having given us Marie de Saint-Pierre. She
was born at Rennes on the 4th of October, 1816. At her baptism she
was given the same patrons as her father and mother— St. Peter, Prince
of the Apostles, and St. Francis of Assisium: Frangoise-Perrine being
derivatives of these names. Her father, Pierre Elnere, was a locksmith
by profession. He married Françoise Portier, who bore him twelve
children. This couple were fervent Christians. The father daily assisted
at Mass, every evening visited the Blessed Sacrament, and during the
day still found time to pray. He early taught his little daughter the
practice of the Way of the Cross, and the mother instilled in her a
tender devotion to the Blessed Virgin. Little Perrine was often sick and
had a disposition difficult to manage. But, thanks to the guidance of
her pious parents, she early learned to govern it and to overcome her
faults. From childhood she had a deep abhorrence of sin and bitterly
reproached herself for the slightest imperfections. Her eldest sister,
finding her one day in tears, asked her the cause of them. "I weep for
my sins," she artlessly answered.

Another day a poor blind man, miserably dressed, passed before
the house. He had lost his way, and paused at the corner of the street,

waiting for some charitable hand to set him right. A secret instinct warned the child that here was an occasion to curb her pride and self-love. Suddenly darting out, she took his arm, and, giving him her hand, she led him whither he wished to go. Whenever anything disagreeable happened to her she checked her impatience, saying: "My God, I offer thee *this* in expiation for my sins."

She had such a dread of evil that, having at the age of eight years an uneasiness respecting a little storybook that had been loaned to her, she carried it to her parish priest and asked his advice. When she learned from him that, without being bad, it was a frivolous book, she immediately returned it without having read the first page. The remembrance of the sufferings of our Lord deeply affected her. She thought her sins were the cause of his sorrows and pains; confused and contrite, she would say: "O my Savior! didst thou see even then, during your Passion, that I would one day be converted and belong entirely to thee?" She often made the Way of the Cross, kissing the earth at each Station. But her chief attraction was mental prayer. At first, not knowing the method, she recited her prayers with great attention, waiting till God should make known to her this holy exercise. She had not long to wait. When she was but ten years old, she heard a sermon on the subject which shed a bright light on her mind and heart, and soon made her proficient in this science of the saints.

At twelve years of age, she lost her mother. Like St. Teresa at the same age and under similar circumstances, she ran in her wild grief to Mary, threw herself at her feet, and implored her to be a mother to her in the place of the one that had been taken from her. The Queen of Heaven adopted, in fact, this innocent soul, and gave her through all her life sensible proofs of her maternal care. As her father was burdened with a large family, he confided her to the care of two aunts, who were persons of great piety. They kept a large store for the sale of seamstresses' work, and had a number of young women in their employ. There Perrine made new progress in virtue, was a model to her companions, and even to several of them became a preceptress of the Interior Life, striving to make them love and practice mental prayer, to be more united to God. She seized every opportunity of devoting herself to works of mercy, such as succoring the poor and visiting and assisting the dying. Near to Mr. Elnere's house a poor family came to live, consisting of three members—the father (a day-laborer), his blind wife, and a little boy four or five years old. The young girl looked upon them as the image of the Holy Family of Bethlehem. She conceived for them a great affection, and spared no care to relieve their poverty; she often visited them, instructed them in their religion, made them approach the Sacraments, and, when there was any disturbance, restored peace in the household. Soon after she devoted herself to nursing a poor young woman, who died in her arms. Receiving her last sigh, she hesitated not with her own hands to prepare her for burial, notwithstanding the fear she had of death, and to which she had never before been in such close proximity.

For a moment, however, this soul so pure was on the point of being seduced by the frivolities of the world. She at first relaxed her fervor and had the misfortune to make a few concessions to vanity. God, in love and mercy, punished her. Pressed by remorse, and having, as a member of the confraternity, to prepare herself for a festival of the Blessed Virgin, she undertook to make a good and serious retreat. She then felt the interior workings of grace, and came forth from these exercises completely changed, resolved more than ever to live for God alone. The desire for a religious life which she had already experienced developed itself strongly in her heart. It was the sole object of her thoughts, of her burning desires. For this end she imposed fasts on herself and made pilgrimages in honor of the Blessed Virgin and St.

Joseph. She also addressed herself to St. Martin, the illustrious Bishop of Tours, for whom she had a great devotion, supplicating him to receive her as a religious in his diocese, though she did not then know that any Carmelites were there.

Still, she was agitated by perplexities. Her confessor, who was a man of God, wished to test her vocation. For five years he made her undergo numerous and painful humiliations. At the end of this time, she was inspired to make a pilgrimage to a celebrated chapel of the Holy Virgin in the vicinity of Rennes—Our Lady of La Peiniere. There she clearly perceived that God called her to serve him by the practice of religious vows. All her yearnings drew her towards Carmel, while her confessor appeared desirous she should enter the order of the Hospital Sisters. But as she was returning from her pilgrimage our Lord, after Holy Communion, made her interiorly hear these words: "My daughter, I *love you too much to abandon you longer to your perplexities. You will not be a Hospitaliere, but a Carmelite.*" The interior voice repeated this several times, "*You will be a Carmelite*"; and she believed the last time was added, "*Carmelite at Tours.*" In the meantime, her confessor, without informing her of the fact, had proposed her as an applicant. Therefore what was her astonishment and joy when she heard him say: "My daughter, you are received among the Carmelites"! She left Rennes on the 11th of November, 1839, under the auspices of St. Martin, whom she had not uselessly invoked. Her virtuous father accompanied and presented her himself. She was then twenty-three years of age.

Chapter 2

Her Mission

In the Carmelite convent Perrine gratefully felt she was in her proper place. The fire of divine love filled her soul. From the first her companions recognized in her a solid judgment united with a cheerful, equable disposition; she was reserved and very discreet; she shunned all self-seeking and singularity; her modesty, mortification, and obedience were most exemplary. The candor and tranquility of her face mirrored the innocence and serenity of her soul. A sweet simplicity characterized this elevated nature, as may be judged by the following trait.

On the day of her arrival, during the hour of recreation, she was invited to sing. Without waiting to be urged, she at once began to sing a canticle which, she says, "I had sung in advance while awaiting the fortunate day of my entrance into Carmel; it commences with these words: 'Blessed be God, I am in a refuge.' . . . They were composed of some fifteen stanzas, and I sang them in so joyous a manner that no one thought of interrupting me." The new-comer did not seem disposed to leave one stanza unsung, when suddenly the Mother-Prioress, at first absent, came in. Finding one singing and the others attentively listening, she judged it a fitting opportunity for giving the new postulant her first trial. "Indeed, you have been

in a hurry," said she to the latter, "to show off your little talent!"
An embarrassing silence followed, which was broken only when the
Mother-Prioress turned to the singer and said: "Let us see if you
know any more." "Oh! yes, Reverend Mother," she answered; "I have
kept the best for you." And without betraying the least annoyance or
ill-nature, she began anew. They knew then that the little girl from
Brittany, by virtue and temperament, was not one ready to take offence
or be easily depressed; that she possessed the cheerfulness which St.
Teresa held as one of the proofs of a vocation to Carmel.

Her first interior attraction was a tender devotion to the Divine
Infancy of Jesus. "I looked on myself," she says, "as a little servant of
the Holy Family, and consecrated myself to them in that capacity."
She mentions having still another ambition, which, with a charming
candor, she thus explains: "The Reverend Mothers were mating their
annual retreat, and during that time the postulants and novices took
their recreation in the novitiate. One evening during recreation, when
we were all collected before a picture of the Holy Family, I proposed
to make a little Bethlehem for the Holy Family, each of us to especially
consecrate ourselves to serve it in the capacity of that beast of burden
which should fall to her lot; for instance, one would represent the ass,
another the ox, and so on. The proposal was unanimously adopted."
The lots were drawn, and, to her great satisfaction, she was chosen to
represent the ass of the Infant Jesus. "Thus," she says, "I was his ass in
prayer, striving to warm him by my love; and his little servant in my
actions, imagining myself in the house of Nazareth, and performing
as if for the Holy Family all the daily duties of my state of life."

She was inspired to honor the Infant Jesus each day of the month by
meditating, one after another, 'on the different mysteries of this period
of his life. Thus the thoughts of the Divine Child followed her in all
her actions, and rendered every occupation easy and agreeable.

On the 8th of June 1811, she made her profession. To the names which she had borne since her novitiate, and which placed her under the protection of the Queen of Angels and the Chief of the Apostles, her devotion for the Holy Family suggested an additional title. Henceforth Perrine Elnere will be known as Sister Marie de Saint-Pierre of the Holy Family.

The Prioress of the Carmelites of Tours at this time was Mother Marie of the Incarnation, a religious as eminent for her prudence as for her exalted virtues. She at once employed the newly-professed in different manual labors and afterwards gave her the office of portress. This office, so contrary to her natural inclinations, was the means Providence used to elevate her to the highest degree of perfection. The pious Sister dreaded its duties, fearing she would not be able to unite with them the spirit of recollection which was so dear to her. Respectfully she made known to the Reverend Mother-Prioress her distaste and fears; notwithstanding which the Mother-Prioress retained her in this employment, and she kept it all her life. This disposition was providential; for thus the humble daughter of the cloister in the performance of her duties frequently found herself in relation with pious secular persons who later on were not slow to aid her in her Work of the Reparation.

This mission, for which, during the four years she had been in the convent, grace was secretly preparing her, was to be conferred on her by our Lord himself. It was the 26th of August 1843, the day after the Feast of Saint Louis, King of France; in the evening the Sister was meditating at the foot of the cross, when the Savior said to her: "I have heard your sighs; I have seen the desire you have to glorify me. *My Name is everywhere blasphemed; even the children blaspheme! This frightful sin more deeply than all others wounds my Divine Heart; by blasphemy the sinner scorns me to my face, openly attacks me, annihilates my Redemption, and pronounces his own condemnation and judgment. Blasphemy is an impoisoned arrow which wounds my Heart continually. I will give you a Golden Arrow, that with the delicious wounds of love you may heal the wounds of malice which sinners give me.*" And he dictated to her the following formula: "May the most sacred, most adorable, most incomprehensible, and most ineffable Name of God be praised, blessed, loved, adored, and glorified in heaven, on earth, and in hell, by all the creatures of God, and by the Sacred Heart of our Lord Jesus Christ in the Most Holy Sacrament of the Altar. Amen."

Such was the *Golden Arrow* that the Lord gave to his servant, assuring her that every time she repeated this formula of praise, she would wound his Heart with a wound of love. "Be watchful of this favor," said he to her; "I shall ask of you an account of it." At that moment it seemed she beheld issuing from the Sacred Heart of Jesus, wounded by this arrow, torrents of graces for the conversion of sinners, which inspired her with confidence to say: "My Lord, dost thou then give me charge of blasphemers?"

She did not fail to make known all this to the Mother-Prioress, who, being as prudent as she was experienced, wished to prove and assure herself it was not an illusion. She consulted pious and learned ecclesiastics, and closely watched the conduct of the Sister. Far from encouraging her in this extraordinary way, she endeavored to turn her from it. She even forbade her to recite certain prayers which had been recommended. But several incidents which she could not but look upon as miraculous—among them her own cure, obtained by the prayers of the Sister in accordance with the order of our Lord, and in the manner he himself willed—decided her to relax her severity towards her and to permit her at least to say the prayers of Reparation.

Our Lord continued to reiterate his orders to his servant. The poor Sister would sometimes exclaim: "Ah! if the Divine Master could suffer bitterness, he would be sorrowful unto death on beholding men, instead of making up for their insufficiency by uniting themselves to him and thus glorifying our Heavenly Father, continually blaspheming his holy Name and united with Lucifer and his reprobates. How satisfied, on the contrary, he would feel to see at least a few faithful and grateful children joined to him to love and bless the Name of that Father whom he so tenderly loves!"

This view of the question brought her to make a heroic act of entire abandonment. "I feel myself," she says, "interiorly urged to make to God the sacrifice of my whole being and all the merits which I can acquire." But she submissively awaited the consent of her Prioress.

On the festival of St. John of the Cross, one of the patrons of Carmel, our Lord made his spouse hear these momentous words: "Till now I have only shown you in part the designs of my Heart, but today I wish to show you them in their entirety. *The earth is covered with crimes. The violation of the first three Commandments of God has irritated my Father; the holy Name of God blasphemed, and the holy day of the Lord profaned, fill the measure of iniquities. These sins have mounted to the throne of God and provoked his wrath, which will soon burst forth if his justice is not appeased. At no time have these crimes ascended so high. I desire, with an ardent desire, that there be formed an association, well approved and organized, to honor the Name of my Father.*"

Here the object of the Work of Reparation is clearly indicated: it is to repair the violation of the first three precepts of the Decalogue, which include all crimes that have a special character of hostility against God and the profanation of the Lord's day.

Amazed and confused, the humble daughter of Carmel hesitated.
But our Lord said to her: "Take good care; for if, wanting in simplicity,
you put obstacles to my designs, you will be responsible for the
salvation of many souls; if, on the contrary, you are faithful, they will
embellish your crown." In conclusion he said: "And to whom should
I address myself, if not to a Carmelite, whose very vocation enjoins on
her the duty of unceasingly glorifying my Name?"

Thirteen days after, on the eve of the Immaculate Conception (7th
of December), the Blessed Savior returned to the same subject, and
this time the culpable nation is named. He made the Sister see how
greatly he was incensed against France on account of her blasphemies.
"He has declared to me," she says, "that he cannot longer dwell in
this France, which, like a viper, tears the bowels of his mercy. He
still patiently bears the contempt shown himself, but the outrages
committed against his Eternal Father provoke his wrath. France has
sucked unto blood the paps of his mercy; this is why justice will now
take the place of mercy, and his wrath burst forth with greater fury for
having been longer delayed. Filled with terror, I tremblingly said: 'My
Lord, permit me to ask if this Reparation which thou desirest be made,
wilt thou yet pardon France?' He answered me: 'I will pardon her *once
more;* but, mark well, *once.* As this crime of blasphemy extends over
the whole kingdom, and as it is public, so also must the Reparation
be public and extend to all her cities. Woe to those who will not make
this Reparation!'"

What Frenchman's heart could hear unmoved warnings so severe,
so solemn? The reproach, alas! is but too well merited, for the
crime is evident and incontestable. Everywhere among us do we hear
incessantly uttered with impunity that blasphemy designated by our
Lord to his servant as a frightful sin. France is pronounced the guiltiest
of all nations, because she is the most highly favored by Heaven, the

most loved of Christ, and the eldest daughter of the Church. Having become in Europe the principal center of the spirit of revolution by the practical atheism she professes in her laws and government, she exerts in regard to blasphemy a kind of universal proselytism, as baneful to individuals as it is to society. Is it astonishing, then, that she is especially threatened with the strokes of Divine Justice? After receiving this communication Sister Marie de Saint-Pierre, as we learn from one of the other Carmelites, came from the choir in a state difficult to describe. She was deathly pale and bathed in tears; her countenance, usually so cheerful, bore an impress of suffering which it long retained. She appeared as if crushed, annihilated beneath the weight of divine wrath.

In the midst of her anguish a great consolation was vouchsafed her. She learned that the Sovereign Pontiff, Gregory XVI, had, by a brief dated August 8, 1843, permitted the establishment of pious Confraternities for the Extirpation of Blasphemy. "I no longer doubted," she says, "that the work entrusted to me came from God. What particularly struck me and awakened my admiration was the following happy coincidence in this manifestation of Divine Providence: On the 8th of August the Sovereign Pontiff issued his brief at Rome, and on the 26th of the same month, and in the same year, the day after the festival of Saint Louis, our Lord revealed to an obscure little Carmelite this great Work in Reparation for blasphemy with which he wished to enrich France as a means of salvation, to snatch her from the hands of his offended and irritated justice."

Chapter 3

HER REVELATIONS ON THE REPARATION

ON Christmas night of 1843, having obtained the permission of her Superiors, the Sister made, according to the reiterated demands of our Lord, "an act placing all her merits in the hands of the Most Holy Infant Jesus." As a reward she was favored with still more abundant lights and graces. "It seems," she says, "that I hear Jesus from the depths of the tabernacle addressing us these words: 'O ye my friends and faithful children, behold if there be any sorrow like unto mine! My Divine Father and my spouse, the holy Church, the delight of my Heart, are despised and outraged by my enemies. Will no one rise up to console me by defending them against those who attack them? I can no longer remain in the midst of this ungrateful people. Behold the torrent of tears that flow from my eyes! Can I find none to wipe them away by making reparation to the glory of my Father and imploring the conversion of the guilty?' Ah!" cries the pious Sister, "if a king, or even his ambassador, be treated with indignity by a foreign power, how quickly the whole nation rushes to arms to avenge the insult! Troops are mustered, and the death of numberless soldiers is accounted as nothing. And yet the holy and terrible Name of the God of hosts, of the King of kings, is despised and blasphemed, his day is profaned by sinners in infinite numbers, and no one is troubled thereat, no one thinks of Reparation. Behold, our Lord Jesus, the Envoy and Son of the God of armies, the Ambassador of the kingdom of heaven, demands a Reparation of honor to his Eternal Father, or war will be declared against us and France will suffer the chastisements of his wrath. Will we pause to weigh the matter? Will we hesitate in our choice?"

The Archbishop of Tours, who at that time was Mgr. Morlot, wished to see and examine the writings of the Carmelite. We say her "writings," because the Mother-Prioress had required her to write all her revelations. The prelate approved in this regard the wisdom of her Superiors, and authorized Rev. Pierre Alleron, Superior of the Carmelites, and at the same time pastor of Notre Dame La Riche, to establish in his parish an Association for the Reparation of Blasphemy. This was on the model of the one in Rome, approved by Gregory XVI August 8, 1843. Its members were thus enabled to gain the numerous spiritual advantages granted to the Roman association. The permission of Mgr. Morlot is dated March 15, 1844. The association, on being established, took for its patrons St. Michael the Archangel, St. Louis, King of France, and St. Martin. Those that belonged to it were to recite daily a *Pater, Ave, Gloria,* and the *Golden Arrow* before mentioned.

This, without doubt, was something— a first step towards the Work of Reparation. But more was required—namely, an archconfraternity similar to that of Our Lady of Victory for the Conversion of Sinners. The Sister was very sorrowful. They saw her coming from her prayers pale, trembling, and bathed in tears. She continually offered herself in sacrifice to turn away the divine scourges and obtain the salvation of her country. On learning that the usual prayer of St. Denis was "Give me souls!" she unceasingly repeated it and begged the Sisters to do the same. In the meantime, the Divine Master revealed to her more and more the enormity of blasphemy.

"You cannot understand," He said to her one day, "the malice and abomination of this sin. If my justice were not restrained by my mercy it would instantly crush the guilty, and all creatures, even inanimate ones, would rise up to avenge my outraged honor." "After this," the Sister adds, "he showed me the excellence of the Work of Reparation; how it surpasses all other devotions, is agreeable to God, to the angels, the saints, and is useful to the Church. Ah! if you knew the degree of glory you acquire in making but a single act of Reparation for blasphemy, in saying only once, in the spirit of Reparation, 'Admirable is the Name of God'!"

She again wrote: "This work is within me as a consuming fire. I continually beg our Lord to deign to save France; to establish in all her cities his Work of Reparation, and to raise up apostolic men for this end. Thou seest, my sweet Jesus, that I, a poor unworthy creature, can do nothing; vouchsafe, then, to enlighten the heart of him who can render thee this service with the knowledge of all that I suffer."

The Carmelites, forced to leave their monastery, lived for two years in a secular dwelling where cloister enclosure was almost impossible. Sister Saint-Pierre, still in her office, of portress of the interior, had much to suffer. But our Lord, in the very midst of the embarrassments and distractions of her charge, consoled her with new and consoling lights. In her great desire to comfort and strengthen those who came to her with their sorrows, she was inspired to communicate to them the devotion of the Gospel of the Circumcision, and of the Holy Name. Thus she writes of this devotion: "The demon uses all possible means to snatch from our Lord Jesus Christ the inheritance purchased by the cross, and he is ever seeking to rob this Good Shepherd of the lambs obtained at so great a price. To put this ravishing wolf to flight Jesus has made known to me that he wishes his sheep marked with his Holy Name, by bearing on their person the Gospel which announces to all nations that the Incarnate Word was named *Jesus*. This amiable Savior has acquainted me with the virtue of his Sacred Name—that it would drive away the demon, and that all those placing themselves under its special protection would receive great graces." Her superiors permitted her to distribute printed sheets of this Gospel on which was stamped an image of the Infant Jesus. To this was added a piece of the palm blessed on Palm Sunday. These sheets were folded and enclosed in a little square sachet, marked upon the outside with the Sacred Heart and the instruments of the Passion. It was to be worn on the person in the same way as a medal attached to a scapular, etc. The pious Carmelite had thus in view the glorification of the Name of Jesus. Numerous graces came to confirm her faith and make her rejoice in the devotion. Everyone wished to have these little sachets. On the sheets, beneath the Gospel, these words were inscribed:

"When Jesus was named,

Satan, vanquished, was disarmed."

"Our Lord has revealed to me," says the Sister, "how glorious it is to him to have his victory celebrated by these words, for they make the demon tremble with rage; that he will bless all who wear this Gospel, and will defend them against the attacks of Satan."

On the 17th of June 1845, the Divine Master resumed his great design, and encouraged his servant to address the archbishop personally. The prelate very kindly visited the holy Carmelite, whose virtues he held in the highest esteem. Ushered into his presence, she knelt, kissed his feet, and humbly asked him to deign to accomplish the work he had so happily begun in authorizing the Association of Notre Dame La Riche; and she disclosed to him how strongly our

Lord had urged her to request the official establishment of the Work of Reparation in the metropolis of Tours, formerly the center of so many graces for France. In the kindest manner the prelate answered: "My child, with all my heart I desire to establish the work and give it all necessary and well-deserved publicity; but there are obstacles in the way which are difficult to overcome. It. is a hard task for us to encourage our people to follow the ordinary practices of piety. Might not the proposal of new and additional devotions provoke the wicked to still greater blasphemy?" Nevertheless, he reassured her by declaring he saw in her revelations no stamp of illusion, but recognized in them the *seal of God;* and he exhorted her to still pray and solicit new light on the subject. He permitted her to recite the prayers of Reparation, and sometime after accorded permission to have them printed. He also approved of a little book on blasphemy entitled *Collection of Prayers,* followed by "Little Office of the Holy Name of God," composed by M. Dupont.

"This little book," says the Sister, "authorized by the archbishop, at once became very popular, and by this means in a short time more than twenty-five thousand Prayers of the Reparation were distributed. Tours received numberless applications for them from persons in various cities who wished to propagate this devotion to the Holy Name of God, and everywhere they were recited with the greatest fervor. Our Lord revealed to me that this new harmony appeased his wrath, but that he still wished to have an association established such as he had demanded."

Chapter 4

HER REVELATIONS ON THE HOLY FACE

OBEYING the archbishop's counsels, Sister Saint-Pierre began to pray with renewed fervor for greater light regarding the establishment of the Work of Reparation. But it pleased the Divine Master to lead his servant once more through the path of interior trials. She was assailed with fears and doubts; terrible temptations met her at every turn; all sensible consolations were withdrawn; she felt that her soul had lost even sanctifying grace, and in her agony she hardly dared receive Holy Communion. One day, while awaiting the hour of Mass, and hesitating as to whether she should approach the holy table, she thought that this Bread of the Strong would infuse courage. She seized with renewed faith her crucifix, and, recalling to mind that Jesus had said that the Act of Praise called the *Golden Arrow* delightfully wounded his Heart, she pronounced this formula ten times in succession and resolved to receive Holy Communion in Separation for blasphemy. Nothing more was needed to touch the Heart of the Heavenly Spouse. This fervent, loving soul was filled with consolations, and the Mystery of the Sorrowful Face of Christ was suddenly revealed to her. She felt herself transported in spirit to the road to Calvary. "There," she says, "our Lord vividly portrayed to me the pious act of Veronica, who with her veil wiped his most Holy Face, covered with spittle, dust, sweat, and blood. This Divine Savior made me understand that the impious at present, by their blasphemies, renewed the outrages formerly inflicted on his Holy Face. All the blasphemies hurled against the Divinity, whom they cannot reach, fall back, like the spittle of the Jews, upon the Face of our Lord, who has offered himself a victim for sinners. Then he told me I must imitate the zeal of the pious Veronica, who so courageously braved the crowd of his enemies to reach him, and he gave her to me as a protectress and model. By promoting the Reparation for blasphemy, we render him the same service as did this heroic Jewish woman, and he looks upon those who thus act with the same complacency as when he gazed upon her on his way to Calvary." All the purpose of the Reparation is here in the germ. We shall behold it developing in the succeeding revelations. Henceforth the Sister applied herself to rendering homage to the Holy Face. "I believe," she says, "I am under the special protection of the pious Veronica; I am continually occupied in adoring the August and Most Holy Face of the Divine Savior. This Adorable Face is the mirror of the perfections contained in the Most Holy Name of God." "I comprehended," she says, "that as the Sacred Heart of Jesus is the sensible object offered to our adoration, to represent his boundless love in the Most Holy Sacrament of the Altar; so in the Work of the Reparation our Lord's Face is the *sensible* object offered to the adoration of the Associates, to atone for the outrages of blasphemers, who attack the Divinity, of which it is the mirror and expression. By virtue of this Adorable Face presented to the Eternal Father we can appease his just wrath and obtain the conversion of the impious and blasphemers." Our Lord favored his servant with still other lights. He made her comprehend that the Church is his mystical body, and religion the face of that body. "He then showed me," she says, "that this face is today a butt for the enemies of his Holy Name; and I saw, by means of this divine light, that the impious, by wicked words and blasphemy against the Holy Name of God, spit upon the Savior's Face and cover it with mud; that all the blows given to Holy Church and religion by sectarians are a renewal of the numerous buffets which the Holy Face of our Lord received, and that these wretches, in striving to annul the infinite merits of its sufferings, cause, as it were, the sweat of this Most Holy Face."

"After this vision," continues the Sister, "the Blessed Savior said to me: 'I seek Veronicas to wipe and honor my Divine Face, which has few adorers.' And he made me understand anew that all who would devote themselves to this Work of the Reparation would thereby perform the office of the pious Veronica. After which he addressed me these words: 'I give you my Face as a recompense for the services you have rendered me. They are slight, it is true; but your heart has conceived great desires. I therefore present you this gift in virtue of the Holy Ghost, in the presence of my Father, the angels and saints, through the hands of my Most Holy Mother and St. Veronica, who will teach you in what manner it should be venerated? He moreover added: 'By my Holy Face you will perform wonders?" The Sister understood that this precious gift was not for herself alone; that it was to become in the Work of Reparation a distinctive sign and powerful means of action. But this grace was for her, after that of the Sacraments, the greatest she could receive. "Now," added the Lord, "if any do not recognize in this my work, it is because they close their eyes."

"Two days after, having taken for the subject of my prayer," the Sister says, "the Betrayal of Judas, I sorrowfully considered the outrage the Face of our Lord had received in the kiss of his perfidious disciple, and it seemed to me that the Divine Master invited me in a spirit

of reparation to kiss most fervently the image of his Holy Face.[1]
After obeying the inspiration I felt that this amiable Savior willed to
instruct me on the excellence of the gift he had presented me in his
Adorable Face, and he had the goodness to accommodate himself to
the feebleness of my mind by the following simple comparison: 'As in
earthly kingdoms,' said he, 'one can obtain what he wills with coin
stamped .with the king's effigy, so with the precious coin of my Sacred
Humility, whose effigy is my Adorable Face, one can obtain in the
kingdom of heaven all that he desires.' And he promised me, besides,
that all who, by words, prayers, or writings, would defend his cause
in this Work of Reparation, he would defend before his Father, and
would give them his kingdom."

Succeeding these communications on the Holy Face, Sister
Saint-Pierre had the next day an interior light on the same subject,
which she expressed in the following prayer:
"Remember, O my soul! the instructions which thy Heavenly Spouse
has this day given thee concerning his Adorable Face. Remember that
the Divine Head represents the Eternal Father, who is unbegotten;
that the mouth of this Holy Face represents the Divine Word,
begotten of the Father; the two eyes, the reciprocal love of the Father
and the Son, for these divine eyes have but one light, one identical
knowledge, and produce the one same love which represents the Holy
Ghost. Contemplate in his flowing hair the infinite perfections of the
Most Blessed Trinity. Behold in this majestic Head, precious portion
of the Sacred Humanity of the Savior, the image of the Unity of God."

A series of other communications soon came to unfold more clearly
these consoling truths. On the 3rd of November, in order to show

---

1. See Brief of Leo XIII

more plainly the propriety of the choice he had made of his Holy Face as the principal object of the Adoration, our Lord declares to Marie de Saint-Pierre that he gives it to her "to be wiped with her homages and perfumed with her praises," and he adds: "According to the care you will take to make reparation to my Face, disfigured by blasphemy, will I take of your soul, disfigured by sin. I will reimprint my likeness upon it and make it as beautiful as when it came forth from the baptismal font. There are men skilled in restoring health to the body, but I alone am the 'healer of souls,' I alone can renew in them the image of God, effaced by sin." Hearing these words, the pious Sister in transports exclaimed: "I salute thee, I adore thee, and I love thee, O Adorable Face of Jesus, my Beloved, noble seal of the Divinity. With all the powers of my soul I apply myself to thee, and I most humbly pray thee to imprint in all of us thy image, disfigured by sin." "What a mystery of love!" continued our Carmelite. "Man is invited to repair the outrages made to his God, and in a loving return he promises to restore his image in our souls! Let us, therefore, wipe the august Face of the Savior, soiled with the spittle of blasphemers, and he will wipe our soul, soiled with the spittle of sin."

Chapter 5

HER PRAYERS FOR FRANCE

The year 1846 had dawned upon the world, and yet there was no outward indication that the ardent wishes of Sister Saint-Pierre would be realized. On the 23rd of January she was favored with a communication which she hastened in tears to make known to the Mother-Prioress. These are the fearful words the Divine Savior used: "The face of France has become hideous in my Father's eyes, and she provokes his justice. To obtain mercy for her, offer him the Face of his Son, in whom he takes complacency. Unless this be done she will feel the weight of his wrath in well-merited chastisements. The Holy Face of her Savior is her salvation. Behold the proof of my goodness to France, who only repays me with ingratitude." Henceforth, docile and frightened, the pious Sister began to say this prayer, which she continually repeated:

"Eternal Father, we offer thee the Adorable Face of thy well-beloved Son for the honor and glory of thy Holy Name and for the salvation of France."

It was now with great anguish that she received new lights. Those warnings of God and the apparent impossibility of seeing his commands obeyed filled her with sorrow and desolation. "My poor heart," she says, "is pierced by a sword of grief. Again has our

Blessed Lord centered all the faculties of my soul upon his precious thorn-crowned Head and his Adorable Face, which is made a butt for the outrages of the enemies of God and his Church. Again have I heard his sorrowful plaints, 'that he seeks souls to atone for the outrages inflicted upon him, and to heal his Divine Wounds by applying to them the wine of compassion and the oil of charity.'"

Four days later the Divine Master made known to his servant that two persons had rendered him signal service during his Passion: the first, as already mentioned, was the pious Veronica, who glorified his humanity by wiping His Adorable Face on the painful road to Calvary; the second was the "good thief," who from his cross, as from a pulpit, openly defended the Savior's cause and confessed his divinity, blasphemed by the other thief and the hardened Jews. He presented both as models in the Work of Reparation—Veronica to those of her own sex who are called to defend his cause, not by preaching, but by wiping his Holy, August Face with the veil of prayer, praise, and adoration; and the "good thief," as the special model of men and the ministers of his Church, who are called upon to publicly defend the honor of God and to proclaim his glory before those by whom it is outraged. To St. Veronica our Lord gave the impression of his divine features; to the "good thief" an immediate entrance into his celestial kingdom. And he promised the Sister to be no less munificent to those who by their "prayers, words, adorations, or writings defended his cause; he will defend their cause before his Father in heaven and give them his kingdom." And he enjoined her to make these promises known to all, adding: "If you keep these things hidden, without speaking of them, you will commit an injustice." In another communication the Lord urged her to offer herself as a victim for the sins of France. "Pray for her," said he; "immolate yourself for her. I give you anew my Face: offer it to my Father to appease his justice. Ah! if you but knew its power, its virtue.

And wherefore? Because I have taken upon my Head all the sins of mankind, in order that my members may be spared. Therefore, offer my Face to my Father, for this is the means of appeasing him." And he added: "I desire the Work of the Reparation; rest assured it will be firmly established, but the fruit you bear is not yet matured."

In the mission assigned to the daughter of Carmel we see the salvation of France closely linked with the Work of Reparation; hence for both our Lord offers the same exterior signs, the same efficacious means—namely, the *cultus* of his Adorable Face. Such is the subject of the following communication: "My daughter, I take you for my steward and anew place my Holy Face in your hands, that you may unceasingly offer it to my Father for the salvation of France. Use to advantage the divine talent which in my Holy Face I entrust to you. By so doing you will obtain the conversion of many sinners. Nothing that you ask in virtue of this offering will be refused you. Ah! if you but knew how pleasing to my Father is the sight of my Face." Again, displaying to her the boundless treasures of the infinite merits of his life and Passion, the loving Savior added: "My daughter, I give you my Face and my Heart, I give you my Blood, I give you my Wounds; draw from them and pour out upon others; buy freely, for my Blood is the price of souls. Oh, what sorrow for my Heart to behold remedies which have cost me so dearly despised by men. Ask of my Father as many souls as I have shed drops of blood in my Passion."

The prayers of Reparation seemed to the Sister a wall which protected France against the shafts of divine justice; a hundred times daily she offered to God the Adorable Face of Jesus.

Another communication, made on the 27th of January 1847, binds together two excellent devotions which in the Work of Reparation occupy an essential place. "Our amiable Savior," says the pious Carmelite, "has made me hear his sighs upon his unappreciated love in the Most Blessed Sacrament of the Altar from the lack of faith among Christians, and he has happily bound my heart and mind at his feet, in order that I may bear him company in this abandonment by adoring his Most Holy Face hidden under the Eucharistic veil. Yes, it is by this august Sacrament that Jesus, our Savior, wishes to communicate to souls the virtue of his Most Holy Face, which is there more dazzling than the sun. And he has promised me anew to imprint on the souls of those that honor it his Divine Likeness."

Then suddenly our Lord gave to her mind a clear perception of the connection existing between his Most Holy Name and His Adorable Face. "He made me understand," says she, "by a comparison as simple as it is appropriate, how the impious, by their blasphemies, attack his Adorable Face, while the faithful glorify it by the homage and praise they render to his Name and his Sacred Person."

"Behold a man, distinguished for his name and merits, in the presence of his enemies; they do not lift a hand against him, but they heap insults upon him, treat him with contempt, and call him by injurious epithets instead of the titles that justly belong to him. Observe now the face of this injured man; does it not seem that all the opprobrious words uttered against him by his enemies are reflected there and make him suffer a veritable torment? See how his face burns with shame and confusion. Is not the ignominy inflicted upon it harder to bear than physical tortures in other parts of his body? This is a faint picture of the Face of our Lord outraged by the blasphemies of the impious!"

"Let us represent to ourselves this same man in the presence of his friends, who, hearing of the insults he has received, hasten to console him by treating him according to his dignity, paying homage to the greatness of his name, and addressing him by all the titles due his exalted rank; does not the face of that man express the sweetness of these praises? Happiness rests upon his brow and beams on his radiant countenance, joy sparkles in his eyes, and a smile is on his lips. In a word, his faithful friends have cured the burning anguish of that Face outraged by his enemies; glory has taken the place of opprobrium. This is what the friends of Jesus do by the Work of Reparation; the glory they render to his Name rests on his august brow and rejoices his Most Holy Face in a special manner in the Blessed Sacrament of the Altar."

In our days the crimes which most outrage our Lord in his Sacraments spring from secret societies. They are designated to the Sister under the general name of *Communists,* as being the greatest enemies of the Church and France. "He has commanded me," she says, "to make war against these wicked men, who for the most part were born in that Church of which they are now the declared enemies. He has given me to combat them the arms of his Passion, his Cross, and the other instruments of his tortures. 'My daughter,' said he, 'they have dragged me from my Tabernacles, they have profaned my Sanctuaries and laid hands on the anointed of the Lord. Have they not committed the crime of Judas? Have they not sold me for money? Let not this knowledge be without fruit. I make it known to you to animate you for the combat. March towards them with the simplicity of a child and the courage of a valiant soldier.'" And the virgin of the cloister repeated with the prophet: "Let God arise and his enemies be dispersed, and let all that hate him flee from before his Face."

This was in 1847. The governments of the period did not appear to be uneasy about the intriguing of these enemies of social order who have since overturned. thrones and brought confusion to Europe. "Alas!" said the pious Carmelite, unable to restrain her tears, "days of wrath are approaching, and yet this Work of the Reparation, which I have borne for nearly four years under sorrows that God, alone can know, has not appeared. O my God! arise; it is thy cause as well as ours; we pray thee to defend France with the protection of thy Holy Face, and grant her mercy for the glory of thy Adorable Name. Yes, enlightened from on high, I firmly believe that on this Work of Reparation depends the future of France. I see it always linked to France as the means of salvation that God in his infinite mercy has chosen for her. Wherefore I would give the last drop of my blood to obtain its establishment, for then the Lord would be appeased, and innumerable souls would be saved."

Chapter 6

THE ARCHCONFRATERNITY OF THE REPARATION

THE 7th of March 1847, our Lord said to his faithful servant: "Rejoice, my daughter; the hour approaches when that most beautiful work under the sun is to appear." As the Sister was much troubled concerning the many obstacles to be overcome, the Divine Savior said to her: "These obstacles are only the mist of a morning ushering in a fine day."

A question rises here regarding the Work of Reparation through the Holy Face. Without doubt the Redemption wrought upon the Cross is, and always will be, the masterpiece of Divine Wisdom and Divine Love; but the Reparation asked by the Savior of Marie de Saint-Pierre is so intimately, connected with the Redemption of man, so identified with the expiation of Calvary, that we may truly consider it an application of the same; and thus, notwithstanding the feebleness and unworthiness of the instruments employed, it is in reality "the most beautiful of works, the most necessary for the needs of the age in which we live."

The day, in fact, was fast approaching when this Work would be definitely established.

The Confraternity not having been instituted at Tours in the manner the Lord wished, the Holy Virgin of La Salette, the 19th of September, came herself in person to begin it. Sister Saint-Pierre had solicited the intervention of Mary, and Mary, our merciful Mother, announced it. "His grace," says Sister Saint-Pierre, "coming to no decision, I appealed to Mary. I clearly saw there was no hope but in her intercession; daily I recited the chaplet to obtain the establishment of the Work. I longed to proclaim it throughout France and make known to my country the misfortunes which threatened her. Oh! how I suffered in being the sole depositary of so important a thing!" "Holy Virgin," she again exclaimed, "appear in the world, make known to some one that which has been communicated to me concerning France." When the pious Sister heard that the august Queen of Heaven had spoken to the little shepherds of the Alps, Maximin and Melanie, in transports she cried: "O Virgin Mother of my God! I thank thee for having given me these two little shepherds as sounding trumpets to echo from the mountain to the ears of France all that has been revealed to me in solitude." And again: "The voice of my dear little associates has been heard throughout the world. Let us pray, let us weep for our sins. The time is not far distant when France will be shaken to her foundations. But she will not be engulfed, if before the eyes of the Lord appears the Work of Reparation. She, who was to be utterly destroyed, will be only lightly chastised." In fact, in less than a year after—and perhaps to this we owe our continued existence—the Work was earnestly begun. Mgr. Parisis, Bishop of Langres, having heard of the projected Work, took a lively interest in forwarding it as much as possible. His zeal for the Holy Name of God made him labor with much ardor for the establishment of the Association; his efforts were crowned with success. He wrote to Mgr. Mor-lot, Archbishop of Tours, who, still judging that it was not opportune to pronounce judgment, left the initiative of the Work to the Bishop of Langres, being all the more willing to do this as Langres was his (Mgr. Morlot's) birthplace. A Confraternity of Reparation was then canonically established at St. Dizier in the church of St. Martin of Lanoue. Reverend M. l'Abbe Marche, its pastor, was sent to Rome to solicit, on behalf of the Association, the title of Archconfraternity, together with some indulgences. Pius IX received the petitions with the most ardent enthusiasm, and it was on this occasion he made use of the words that have been so often quoted: "Reparation is a work destined to save society." He granted the requested indulgences, and by a brief dated July 30, 1847, raised the Association of Reparation established at St. Dizier to the dignity of an Archconfraternity, with the right of aggregating throughout the Catholic world similar associations; and His Holiness requested that his name should be the first subscribed on the register of membership— a signal privilege, which was to be the seed of wonderful benedictions.

The Confraternity of the Reparation answered so well the need of our times, and was so evidently the work of God, that from its very commencement it spread like a fire among dry reeds.

Nevertheless it had for its center only the second parish of a small town, in a, diocese far from the place where the communications had been made. Besides, the episcopal ordinance of Langres had made no mention of the *cultus* of the Holy Face indicated as the sensible object of the Reparation. Consequently, though the canonical erection of the Archconfraternity of the Reparation filled the pious Sister with joy, she yet said, "My heart is not entirely satisfied; for in this work the Church of Tours, the heritage of the great St. Martin, still remains inactive. When will it bring forth the fruit which has been conceived in its midst?"

She was not to see the fulfilment of this legitimate desire; her earthly pilgrimage was drawing to a close. Still the future welfare of her country was ever before her, and she ceased not most earnestly to pray for its salvation.

On the 2nd of December our Lord appeared to her covered with wounds. "He made me," she says, "hear these sorrowful words: '*The Jews crucified me on Friday; but the Christians crucify me on Sunday*'. Ask them in my name, at least for this diocese of Tours, the establishment of the Work of Reparation, in order that my friends may embalm my Wounds by pious expiations and obtain mercy for the guilty. My daughter, the storm is already threatening, but I shall keep my promise if my wishes be accomplished. Speak with humility and at the same time with holy liberty.'"

The storm of which the Savior spoke was indeed at hand. Two months later it was to burst forth in all its fury. This the Divine Master clearly announced to his servant in a communication of the 13th of February.

"Our Lord," she says, "has made known to me in these words the terrible woes impending over us: '*The Church is threatened with a fearful tempest. Pray, pray!*' It is impossible," she adds, "to describe the touching and impressive accents with which this charitable Savior said to me, 'Pray, pray!'"

This prediction was, indeed, verified in 1848, in the epoch usually called *Days of February,* by an unexpected Revolution which hurled Louis Philippe from his throne, made France a Republic, and shook all Europe, particularly Rome, which Pius IX was obliged to leave and seek refuge in Gaeta.

The soul of the Sister was in anguish. "Ah!" she cried, "the Lord has long asked of France a Work which would be for her *a rainbow of mercy*. Happily, the work has been inaugurated, and its influence is being felt; but it is yet too feeble to arrest the wrath of the Omnipotent. Ah! if it were but extended to all the dioceses I should be without uneasiness, for God is faithful to his promises." She adds: "Oh! how I wish to make known to all the bishops this consoling truth and entreat them in this great crisis to aid in the Work of Reparation. I have always said it, and I again repeat it: *It is this Work which is to disarm the justice of God and save France and the world!* Happy if they know how to profit by this means of salvation!"

"Nothing," she further says, "is more efficacious to disarm the irritated justice of God than to offer him this Most Holy Face, which has taken upon its Head the thorns of our sins and has exposed itself to the strokes of that same justice. It has cancelled our debts, it is our security; whence our amiable Savior has commanded me, notwithstanding my unworthiness, to keep myself constantly before the throne of his Father, offering him this Divine Face, the object of his complacency. And this tender Savior has made me the consoling promise: 'Every time you offer my Face to my Father, I will open my Mouth to demand mercy.' The good Jesus has also promised to have pity on France. Let us, then, have great confidence; his all-powerful Name will be our buckler, and his Adorable Face our rampart. And he made me also understand that he wished this devotion to his Adorable Face rapidly and widely extended. O good Jesus! hide us in the secret of thy Holy Face, that it may be for us an impregnable tower, a fortress against the attacks of our enemies." One day after Holy Communion our Lord appeared in the interior of her soul as he is represented in the *Ecce Homo.* "He at first attracted my attention," she says, "upon the contemplation of his Holy Face. Soon he directed it to the reed he held in his Hand and presented it to me to combat the enemies of the Church, promising me they would feel my blows.

He made me understand that this feeble reed was the figure of my soul. Yes, I am only a feeble reed, but in the Hand of Jesus Christ, my Spouse, becoming most powerful against his adversaries, I shall say with faith and confidence: 'O malice of the demon, vanish before the reed of Jesus Christ!'

"Eternal Father, I offer thee the Most Holy Face of Jesus. It is a mysterious coin of infinite value which alone can cancel our debts. Eternal Father, I offer thee the Most Holy Face of Jesus to appease thy wrath. Remember it has borne the thorns of our sins, and the blows of thy justice, of which it still bears the marks. Behold those Divine Wounds of whose voice I wish to be the echo; they incessantly cry, 'Mercy, mercy, mercy for sinners!'"

With these words she bowed her face to the earth, saying; "Lord, I merit only hell!" The Good Master answered: "I have applied to your soul the virtue of my Face, to restore therein the image of God. Those who will contemplate the wounds of my Face on earth shall one day contemplate it radiant with glory in heaven."

"At that moment," says the Sister, "I was on Thabor and would fain have repeated with the Apostle St. Peter: 'Lord, it is good to be here. Let us make three tabernacles for the three powers of my soul, that it may always enjoy this sweet repose which infinitely surpasses all the pleasures of earth.' But our Lord made me understand that his true spouses should prefer the heat of combat to the repose of contemplation and should not shrink from throwing themselves into the conflict to defend his glory."

It was after these divine consolations that Marie de Saint-Pierre composed as by inspiration those beautiful invocations of the "Adorable Face of our Lord" improperly called the "Litany." They are jets of light, cries of love, a kind of spiritual poem to the glorification of the Holy Face, which she is pleased to consider under its different aspects—joyous, sorrowful, glorious, merciful, and terrible. At the end of her writings, in a hymn of thanksgiving, she particularly thanks our Lord "for having made her the gift of his Divine Face, so suitable to appease the justice of the celestial Father, and from which flows a precious Blood which assures us of eternal life." She adds: "O blessed, holy angels! thank Jesus and Mary for me, who have heaped favors upon me, and draw me to heaven, in order that I may, notwithstanding my unworthiness, sing eternally with you a hymn of gratitude for all the graces I have received from my God, and, above all, for the Work of Reparation which his mercy has established in France."

Chapter 7

HER VIRTUES

IT is time to speak a few words of the virtues of our dear revered Sister. We shall only mention those which were the most characteristic.

Above all, she possessed charity in an eminent degree; the glory of God and the conversion and salvation of sinners were the sole objects of her thoughts and the motive of all her actions. The loss of souls made so vivid an impression upon her that she could not repress her sorrow. More than once she was heard weeping and sobbing. Her tender and solid piety also inspired her with a great zeal to relieve the souls in purgatory, especially those that were the most forlorn.

Her heart expanded with love for our Lord; she honored his Sacred Humanity in all its mysteries, but those of his Birth and Hidden Life had for her inexpressible charms. Her devotion to the Divine Infancy and to the Holy Family was manifest on all occasions. Being Portress, it was a source of joy to her to open the door to carpenters, whose occupation reminded her of the labors of the childhood of Jesus and St. Joseph. One day a wagon drawn by an ass entered the courtyard of the monastery. Approaching the animal, the good Sister began to tenderly stroke it in remembrance of the service rendered Jesus and Mary by the humble beast in their flight into Egypt. At

Christmas-time she testified her joy and piety in various ways; she contemplated with a radiant countenance the statue of the Infant Jesus in the Crib, took it in her arms, lighted tapers before it, and sang for the Divine Babe her sweetest songs of praise; sometimes, even, like David before the Ark, she began to dance, inviting her companions in the Novitiate to do the same. The Mother-Prioress expressed astonishment and warned her against dissipation. "Oh! no, Reverend Mother," she answered. "I do it to honor the Infant Jesus, and to make amends for all the guilty dances that offend him."

Her affections were also directed to Jesus in the Eucharist. In the choir, before the Blessed Sacrament, the expression of her face, her manner, her looks, made it seem that, piercing the Eucharistic veil, she really saw Jesus on the altar. Quitting the sanctuary, she left there her heart; and in whatever part of the house, she happened to be, she turned towards it, transported with joy when she could catch a glimpse of the altar. She had attained to a rare degree of humility. She sincerely believed herself the least in the community, the most miserable, an unworthy sinner, and reproached herself for the slightest imperfections as if they were grave faults. One day a Sister found her weeping and asked the cause. Sister Saint-Pierre reminded her of a fault she had committed the day previous in her presence. The Sister assured her she had not noticed it, it was so very trifling. "Nevertheless," she answered, "God may have been offended, and that is the cause of my tears." Self-complacency found no place in her mind. She ingenuously avowed it. Once, when she was still a novice, the Mother-Prioress during recreation asked her to sing for a newly-arrived postulant the canticle, "Blessed be God, I am his spouse." She did so with so sweet a voice and so lively an accent of piety that her young companion was delighted. When she had finished the Mother-Prioress said aloud: "Eh, well, my Sister Saint-Pierre, how many thoughts of vanity had you whilst singing?" Lowering her eyes, she modestly answered: "If I have had any I have banished them."

Her obedience was prompt, implicit, and perfect. She complied in the simplicity of a child with all that was required, stimulated thereto by the example of the Child Jesus at Nazareth. The words of the Gospel, "He *was submissive to them*" were ever on her lips. She rendered a blind obedience not only to her superiors, but to the Sisters upon whom she was dependent, and, in fact, to all, regarding them as her mistresses and making it a duty to acquiesce in their wishes, just like a child who has no will but that of its guardians. Thus, she was able in her last sickness to say in all truth and candor: "It is my consolation in death that I have always been obedient."

Her recollection was so profound that merely to see her was sufficient to raise one's thoughts to God. She seemed unconscious of what was going on around her, so much so that even after her Profession she was ignorant of the various places assigned the different nuns in the choir and refectory. One of the nuns, whose cell was so situated that she had an opportunity of seeing her when she thought herself unseen by human eye, assures us that during the time she occupied this cell, which was for several years, she never saw her raise her eyes from her work but to cast them on the little statue of the Infant Jesus which she always kept near her.

After any supernatural communications she would appear pale, trembling, and bathed in tears; especially was this the case when they revealed the woes impending over France. Then her tears flowed, yet calmly and silently. She would then appear so absorbed in recollection that it was difficult to draw her therefrom; and this would last for hours, though without hindrance to the performance of her duties. Her union with God was intimate and continual; she never lost sight of him, and, according to her expression, her soul, closely united to our Lord, was "happily bound at his feet." But this life, apparently so heavenly and sweet, was not exempt from interior trials and sufferings. The Mother-Prioress was convinced that these were so great that, whilst serving to purify her soul, they shortened her days in this world.

She also possessed in an eminent degree that sweet liberty of spirit which distinguishes a true Carmelite. She knew perfectly well how to blend with the practice of the most exalted virtues the charms of charity, and even gayety. One day a friend brought to the convent as a present a piece of cake. Sister Saint-Pierre, then Portress, was very fatigued. On receiving the cake she immediately carried it to the Mother-Prioress, and, presenting it to her, said with her usual simplicity: "What a providence—the ass of the Infant Jesus is hungry!" The good Mother smiled and gave a piece of the cake to her little Portress, who, giving thanks to God, gaily partook of it.

During recreations she spoke but little, always preferring to listen; nevertheless, she was cheerful and amiable, expressing herself to the point and taking part in all that was said, though it was often necessary for her to make extremely violent efforts to break off her interior converse with God. Her companions loved to be near her, because they always found it to their spiritual benefit. Her reserve was especially noticeable in matters pertaining to charity; she excused everyone, palliated their defects, and this with tact and cordiality.

During her last illness, having passed a night of extreme suffering, she said to a nun who was from the same part of the country as herself: "You remember that in Brittany our little excursions ended with a feast, each person furnishing his or her share, one paying for the cream, another for the sugar. The good Jesus last night assigned to me the furnishing of the sugar by making me suffer very much."

When, in 1848, she fell sick, it was at the time of the government elections, and the Carmelites had had more than one alarm. One day the Mother-Prioress said half-jestingly: "Since you cannot pray any more, you will be the spiritual drum, and whenever you hear the National Guard beat the call to arms, do you call the holy angels to our assistance." She accepted her new mission, and the next day presented the Reverend Mother with a little drum, upon which was inscribed the Holy Name of God and that of each of the choirs of holy angels. Unable to make vocal prayers, she would take the little drum on her bed, and, striking it with her fingers, thus call the heavenly militia to their aid. The world may laugh at this trait of childish piety, but those not of the world will see in it the admirable simplicity of a soul transformed by the science of the Crib and the virtue of obedience. This drum, after the death of the Sister, was sent to a friend of Carmel as a plaything to amuse his little boy. But in his family it was richly encased under a glass globe and is preserved as a precious relic.

Until the last our dear Sister cherished a special devotion to the Divine Infant Jesus and the cares which at that period of his life he received from his august Mother. She was richly rewarded by the ineffable communications graciously vouchsafed to her concerning the Divine Maternity, whence she drew greater and still greater confidence for the triumph of the Church and the salvation of France.

Chapter 8

HER LAST SICKNESS -- HER DEATH

THE mission of the Sister was accomplished. According to the designs of God there remained for her but to perfect the sacrifice which she had so often made of herself. Already her health was beginning to fail. At the close of the Lent of 1848, she entered upon those sufferings which, uniting her more and more to Jesus Crucified, were to crown her pure, holy life by an admirable death.

On Good Friday, at three o'clock, when prostrate on the ground adoring Jesus Christ dying on the Cross, it was revealed to her that the divine wrath was about to descend upon men.

Immediately, renewing her act of perfect abandonment, she offered herself to God as a victim to appease his irritated justice. It seemed as if the Lord had awaited this last and generous offering before immolating his courageous victim, for immediately was developed that long and painful sickness which caused her final dissolution. She was consumed by a burning fever; her throat became ulcerated; her tongue and mouth were as if incessantly pierced by cruel thorns—a noticeable fact, since our Lord had told her she must pray and suffer for blasphemers. Night after night she was unable to take the slightest repose; each change of position on her bed became a new martyrdom;

ulcers were formed, which added to her suffering. This frightful state for human nature she bore without the least injury to her interior disposition; her patience never waned, her union with God was continual, her spirit of sacrifice entire and without reserve, her docility, innocence, and simplicity like that of a child.

Early in June she received the Holy Viaticum and Extreme Unction with a fervor and rapture that made it seem that she already had a foretaste of the eternal joys in store for her. On Friday, the 16th of June, they thought her dying and began the Prayers for the Agonizing. Perfectly conscious, she united with the pious nuns by making frequent aspirations. Suddenly she entered into a supernatural state, the effects of which were very apparent. When, after the recommendations of the departing soul, they pronounced these words, *"Maria, mater gratiae, mater misericordiae"* she impulsively threw up her arms toward heaven with the eagerness of a child at the sight of its mother. She remained a long time in this position, although a few moments before so weak and stiff were her arms that they seemed immovable. Afterwards she extended them in the form of a cross, to expire as a victim. When the dear nuns attempted to prevent it she said: *"Leave me thus; for me it is a duty."* Alternately taking her crucifix and the little statue of the Infant Jesus which never quitted her, she covered them with kisses and pressed them to her heart. Then, holding the little statue as high as possible, she pronounced in a low, solemn tone these words: "Eternal Father! once more I offer this Adorable Child, thy Divine Son, in expiation of my sins and those of the human race, for the needs of the Holy Church, for France and the Reparation. Amiable Jesus, I abandon this work into thy hands; for it I have lived, for it I shall die." Then, placing the statue on her head, she said: "Divine Child, cover my criminal head with the merits of thy Precious Blood; renew in my soul grace and innocence; clothe me in thy purity and the spirit of thy humility. Oh! hasten unto me! When shall I leave earth? Come, O my Jesus, and delay not! Mary, my tender Mother, come for my soul!"

She said to the Mother-Prioress: "My career is finished, as our Lord has made known to me; for the Work of Reparation which is to save Prance is established. It was for this God placed me on earth. Now I have but to suffer; it is necessary for the accomplishment of his designs. Ah! how true it is that he has means of satisfying his justice unknown to man."

Her agony was long and painful. As death approached she recollected that our Lord had promised to restore to her soul at the last hour the image of God, and she wished to renew her baptismal vows; as a symbol of the grace she desired to receive, she asked for some holy water, made the sign of the cross upon her head, and pronounced these words: " Child, I baptize thee in the Name of the Father, and of the Son, and of the Holy Ghost." Then, joining her hands, she added: "I renounce Satan and all his works and pomps; I desire to belong for ever to Jesus Christ." After this little ceremony her face assumed such an expression of heavenly beauty that one might readily have imagined her a child just from the waters of Baptism or an angel about to re-ascend to its celestial home. From that moment till her last sigh, she never ceased praying. The sweat of death covered her brow, its chill had already benumbed her pain-worn frame, and yet the cold, livid lips continued to murmur: "Jesus, Mary, Joseph! Come, Lord Jesus! *Sit Nomen Domini benedictum!*" These were her last words. Soon her eyes closed, and, as a last trait of resemblance to her Divine Master, she uttered a cry, and sweetly expired. It was on Saturday, a day consecrated to Mary. The mortal remains of this admirable daughter of St. Teresa have been, through the care of M. Dupont, deposited within the enclosure of the Carmel of Tours, in the Chapter-Hall where they now repose, which corresponds to that part of the chapel which is on the right of the entrance. A mural stone near the holy water font bears this simple inscription:

Here rests
Sister Marie de Saint-Pierre of the Holy Family,
A Professed Religious of this Monastery,
Who died July 8th, 1848,
Aged 31 years and 9 months,
Having been a Religious 9 years and 8 months.
Lord, thou wilt conceal her in the secret of thy Face.

Chapter 9

THE CONFRATERNITY OF THE HOLY FACE

A FTER the death of Sister Saint-Pierre two works, closely allied in spirit to the Reparation and the Adoration of the Holy Sacrament, came from her virginal tomb like two miraculous flowers — the Congregation devoted to Perpetual Adoration, founded by Mlle. Dubouche, in religion Mother Mary Teresa; and the Nocturnal Adoration by men, inaugurated by the celebrated Jew pianist, Hermann, later Father Marie-Augustine, of the Order of Discalced Carmelites. But it was M. Dupont who, in the designs of God, had the special mission to carry out and develop the work shown to the Carmelite of Tours for the salvation of France: the Work of Reparation for blasphemy and the profanation of Sunday by the *cultus* of the Holy Face.

Towards the close of the Lenten season of 1851 he exposed in his private oratory an engraving of the Sorrowful Face of our Lord, an authentic *facsimile* of the Veil of Veronica preserved in the Vatican Basilica. Miracles ere long became manifest. The man of God rejoiced, because he beheld in them a proof of the truth of the revelations made to Sister Marie de Saint-Pierre. To the end he hoped the life and writings of the venerable Sister would be published. Understanding their worth, he knew how much good they would effect. His hope was realized. In 1876, before his earthly career ended, he learned that the Archbishop of Tours, Mgr. Colet, had issued orders that insured their being presented to the world. With a radiant face he blessed God, and, with his gaze turned towards the Carmelite convent, peaceably expired on the 18th of March. On his death his oratory, where for twenty-five years the Holy Face had been honored, was at once transformed into a public chapel. Mgr. Colet officiated on the occasion of its dedication. At the same time he established in this sanctuary the Confraternity of the Reparation for Blasphemy and for the Profanation of Sunday, affiliating it to that of St. Dizier already erected. Using his power as Ordinary, he gave to this Confraternity of Tours a distinct character, and made of it, properly speaking, a Confraternity of the Holy Face, which was really the embodiment of Sister Saint-Pierre's inspirations. Finally, to minister to the new chapel and attend to the spiritual wants of the pilgrims who flocked from all parts thither, the worthy successor of St. Martin instituted, under the title of "Priests of the Holy Face," a society of regular clergy living in community in the house formerly occupied by M. Dupont, and who, following in his footsteps and under his auspices, would devote themselves to all the Works of Reparation.

Since then the Oratory of the Holy Face has become a center of prayers and expiations to which the gaze and hearts of numbers turn, not only from all parts of France, but, in truth, from all Christendom.

Nor was it long before other Confraternities of the Holy Face, similar to the one founded at Tours by Mgr. Colet, were established in many cities. Letters from all parts of the world are received soliciting pictures of the Holy Face like the one so long venerated by M. Dupont, which was an authentic fac-simile of the Veil of Veronica. It would be impossible to calculate the number of the holy pictures exposed in various places (and nearly always with a lamp burning before them)—in cathedrals, parish churches, public chapels, private houses and oratories, in hospitals, and in the enclosure of religious communities. The Priests of the Holy Face at Tours have charged themselves with the pious duty of obtaining these pictures (the fac-simile of Veronica's Veil) from Rome and facilitating their distribution, or rather, we should say, supplying the demand for them, which is a consequence of the recognition of the wants of our age; so natural is the idea of Reparation, so befitting and salutary, so powerful in attracting souls.

This need of Reparation is urgent; all Catholic hearts welcome its appearance. If it be true that France, God's privileged nation, the Eldest Daughter of the Church, be the most guilty, because "much shall be demanded from her to whom much has been given"; that blasphemy in her midst is more audacious, and profanations of God's Holy Days more perverse; should not every generous Christian soul feel called upon to labor zealously in establishing and propagating this Work of Reparation so urgently demanded, in our Lord's Name, by the Carmelite of Tours? What is more natural and just than to unite our efforts in repairing what impiety and hatred of God have combined to corrupt and ruin? The Work revealed to the admirable virgin whose history has been related is at the same time, as she herself says, "a necessity of justice and a pledge of mercy." Let our efforts be in common, let us unite ourselves in striving fervently to appease Divine Justice; then it will be our consolation to experience, only the effects of mercy, which will be all the more abundant as our Reparation has been prompt and fervent.

CONDITIONS

For being deceived into the Confraternity of the Reparation of the Holy Face.

1. To be inscribed on the Register of the Confraternity where it is canonically established.

2. To obtain a copy of the Regulations, wherewith will be found the ticket of admission.

3. To wear at all times the Cross of the Confraternity.

4. Never to blaspheme, and to do all one can to prevent blasphemy.

5. When not possible to prevent these crimes, to make, at least, an interior act of Reparation for them.

6. To recite daily a *Pater, Ave,* and *Gloria Patri,* "with the Act of Praise," in union with the Associates, in the spirit of Reparation.

Note.—The Most Reverend Archbishops, Right Reverend Bishops, and Reverend Clergy, also all pious laymen, are earnestly requested to use their influence in having exposed for devotion pictures of the Holy Face, and establishing everywhere the Confraternity of the Reparation for Blasphemy and Profanation of Sunday.

All desired information connected with this Confraternity may be obtained by addressing the Reverend Director of the Confraternity, Oratory of the Holy Face, 8 Rue Saint-Etienne, Tours, Indre-et-Loire, France; or the Reverend Mother-Prioress, Convent of Discalced Carmelites, 134 Barrack Street, New Orleans, Louisiana, in whose chapel the Confraternity of the Holy Face is canonically established.

APPENDIX

CONTAINING RULES, PRAYERS & DEVOTIONS FOR THE CONFRATERNITY OF THE HOLY FACE

I. H. S.

True Image of the Holy Face of our Lord Jesus Christ, Religiously venerated and kept in Rome, in the Basilica of Saint Peter, in the Vatican.

RULES

OF THE

Confraternity of Reparation

IN HONOR OF

THE HOLY FACE.

NEW ORLEANS, LA.
1883.

Historical Notice

P ius IX, in an audience of July 30, 1847, approved the Confraternity for the Reparation of Blasphemy and the Profanation of Sunday. His Holiness greeted the petition with the most ardent enthusiasm, requested that his name be the first inscribed on the register of the Confraternity, and said that the "Reparation was a work destined to save society." Sister Saint-Pierre, on hearing this, exclaimed: "My mission here below is accomplished; I can now die!" She died a year later, July 8, 1848.

M. Dupont developed and continued her "work." On Wednesday of Holy Week (1851) he lighted a lamp (which has never ceased to burn night and day) before the image of the Holy Face, which is the sensible sign of the Confraternity of the Reparation. The miraculous graces obtained by the oil of the I lamp were to his eyes as so many proofs that our Lord accepted the devotion rendered to his Holy Face as a means of repairing the outrages committed I against the majesty of the Thrice Holy Name of God. He never ceased to recommend the Reparation. He said: "Pray that this work may spread. It seems from what is taking place that our Lord desires, and without delay, that souls devoted to him should practise this salutary exercise. It is a necessity that those who comprehend what God wills should courageously walk in the way of Reparation."

The work has spread, and today the members in the different parts of the world are counted by hundreds of thousands. In transforming the oratory of M. Dupont into a public chapel Msgr. Colet, Archbishop of Tours, erected there June 2, 1876, a Confraternity of Reparation in honor of the Holy Face; also established a society of priests who would devote themselves to it and extend its propagation.

"Our Lord," said Sister Saint-Pierre, "demands this work of Reparation of France which will be a *rainbow of mercy*. Ah!" said she, "if it were established in all dioceses I would be without uneasiness, for God is faithful to his promises. ... Oh! how I would wish to make known to all bishops this consoling truth and ask them with earnest supplication the establishment of this work of the Reparation! I have always said it, and I now repeat it, *This work will disarm the anger of God, save France and the world.*"

Happy are those who profit by this means of salvation.

Rules of the Confraternity of the Holy Face

In Reparation for Blasphemy and the Profanation of Sunday.

Established at Tours in the Oratory of the Venerated M. Dupont, and in the Chapel of the Disealced Carmelites, New Orleans.

Article 1. The end of the Confraternity of the Reparation in honor of the Holy Face is, 1st, to repair the outrages committed against the Divine Majesty of God by blasphemies, the profanation of Sunday and the feasts of the Church; 2nd, to obtain the conversion and salvation of blasphemers and profaners; 3rd, to preserve youth and the family from the fatal effects of these scandals.

To obtain this triple end, so important in our day, it proposes to render a special *cultus* of prayer, adoration, and love to the most Holy Face of our Lord, outraged and disfigured in his Passion.

Art. 2. It is consecrated to the Adorable Trinity, to the Holy Name of Jesus, and to his Sorrowful Face.

It is placed under the patronage of St. Michael, St. Martin, and St. Louis, protector of France. In the cultus which the Confraternity renders to the Holy Face it takes for its models the Immaculate Virgin

Mary, patroness of the United States; the Apostle St. Peter, and the pious Veronica. Trinity Sunday is the principal feast; the second one is that of the Holy Name of Jesus, the second Sunday after Epiphany; and for particular feasts those of the saints above mentioned or those who are proposed as models.

Art. 3. Catholics of all ages, of either sex, and of all conditions are exhorted to enter this Confraternity. Children who have not yet made their first Communion will be received as aspirants and placed most particularly under the protection of the Amiable Face of the Saviour, who so tenderly called little children to Him.

Art. 4. Each member from the time of entrance into the Confraternity devotes himself for life and death to the worship of the Merciful and Compassionate Face of our Lord, and assumes the strict obligation never to utter blasphemies or imprecations, to hold no conversation, to read nothing written, and to take no part in any act which outrages God and our Lord Jesus Christ in his saints or through his works; never to perform any servile work on Sundays and holidays without necessity and without permission.

Art. 5. Those in authority over others, such as parents, public men, masters, superintendents of works, patrons, workmen, etc., should make a firm resolution as far as is in their power to promote the observance of the rules which are laid down in the preceding Article. They will take particular care that the aspirants of the Confraternity shall not receive scandal in this, regard.

Art. 6. When the members hear a blasphemy or any impious word uttered, when they see Sundays and holidays profaned and cannot prevent it, they should offer up to God some Reparation, saying, for example, *Sit Nomen Domini benedictum*—May God be praised; may his Holy Name be blessed; Our Father, hallowed be thy Name; God our Protector, look upon the Face of thy Christ. They may also add *Vade retro, Satana.*

Art. 7. The Confraternity of the Reparation considers the Adorable and Sorrowful Face of our Lord the exterior sign and sensible object of the Reparation, as has been declared by the ordinance, dated June 2, 1876, of his Grace the Archbishop of Tours, who canonically erected the said Confraternity in "the oratory of M. Dupont. There since 1851 has been honored a picture of the Face of our Lord, an authentic *facsimile* of the celebrated Veil of the Vatican, given to the servant of God by the Rev. Mother-Prioress of the Carmelites on account of his zeal for the Reparation and in remembrance of the pious relations he had with Sister Saint-Pierre, who died in the odor of sanctity July 8, 1848."

This sign is represented by a Cross, on one side of which is an image of the Holy Face, bearing on the top the inscription of the cross, on either arm "Tours, 1876," at the base "Vade retro, Satana," on the reverse side the monogram of Christ encircled by these words, "Reparation, Pius IX., 1847," and upon the Cross, "Sit Nomen Domini Benedictum."

Art. 8. The members will recite daily a Pater Noster, Ave Maria, Gloria Patri, and the Act of Praise in Reparation for outrages committed against God by blasphemy and the profanation of Sunday; they will at least unite their intention to the prayers which are offered up daily in the oratories of Reparation, in the morning after the 7 o'clock Mass and in the afternoon at 5 o'clock. The Litany of the Holy Face, composed by Sister Saint-Pierre and approved by ecclesiastical authorities, is daily recited in the oratories, after which follow the different recommendations presented by the faithful.

Art. 9. On the last Sunday of every month, in the afternoon, a solemn assembly takes place in the oratories of the Holy Face, in reparation for these same outrages, but more especially for those committed within the month. The Act of Reparation is recited with the invocations: St. Michael, pray for us; St. Peter, pray for us; St. Martin, pray for us; St. Louis, pray for us; O God our Protector! look upon the Face of thy Christ and we shall be saved. These prayers are preceded by an Instruction and followed by Benediction of the Blessed Sacrament.

Each member is exhorted to offer up these prayers every other Sunday of the month in reparation for the sins of each week.

On the first Thursday of the month the evening assemblies, held at 5 o'clock, are specially devoted to the aspirants of the Work of Reparation.

(Special prayers are also recited daily, weekly, and monthly in the chapel of the Discalced Carmelites for the Reparation of the evils of this country—namely, intemperance, gambling, immorality, etc.)

Art. 10. The director of a canonically- established Confraternity admits as members those who ask to have their names inscribed upon the register. All are exhorted to habitually wear the Cross of the Confraternity and to read over the Rules from time to time. To share in the merits of the work the name must be inscribed in the register. A particular register is kept for the aspirants of the work who, after their first Communion, may desire to have their names inscribed in the grand register.

Art. 11. The Confraternity of Reparation established at Tours and in the Carmelite chapel, New Orleans, La., are canonically affiliated to the Archconfraternity of St. Dizier, diocese of Langres, and enjoy the same privileges and spiritual favors.

Art. 12. The members may gain the following *Plenary* and *Partial* Indulgences:

Plenary: 1st. On the day of admission and putting on the Cross. 2nd. At the hour of death. 3rd. On the feasts of the Holy Trinity, the Holy Name of Jesus, St. Michael, St. Martin, and St. Louis, either on the day itself or on any day during the octave (Pius IX, July 27, 1847). 4th. On the last Sunday of each month, if they assist at the monthly meeting and if the Cross of the Confraternity is worn habitually (applicable to the souls in Purgatory—Pius IX., Aug. 18, 1847).

(To gain the foregoing Indulgences it is necessary to go to Confession and Holy Communion, visit an oratory of the Confraternity (or, if this is impossible, one's parish church), and there pray for the intentions of the Sovereign Pontiff.—Pius IX, Aug. 18, 1848.)

Partial Indulgences; 1st. 100 days for each pious work of the Confraternity (Pius IX, July 27, 1847); 2nd. 300 days for attending the monthly meeting (applicable to the souls iii Purgatory—Pius IX, Aug. 18, 1848); 3rd. 100 days for every prayer offered before an image of the Holy Face (applicable to the souls in Purgatory—Pius IX, Dec. 11, 1876); 4th. 40 days for attending each of the Exercises of Reparation which are held morning and evening in the oratories of the Holy Face (Archbishop of Tours, Nov. 15, 1876).

These Rules of the Confraternity in Reparation for Blasphemy and the Profanation of Sunday, canonically erected at Tours and New Orleans in honor of the Holy Face, have been seen and approved.

Tours, Nov. 15, 1876.

Charles, *Archbishop of Tours.*

New Orleans, March 12, 1883.

N. J. Perche,
Archbishop of New Orleans,

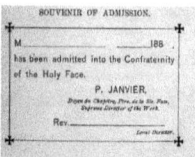

Forms for the Canonical Erection of the Confraternity in a Parish Church or Chapel.

Reverend pastors, chaplains, almoners, superiors or directors of communities should—

1. Ask the permission of the ordinary and his approval of the Rules.

2. Adopt the Rules used by the Confraternity established at Tours, with any special modifications the ordinary may see fit to suggest.

3. Obtain a diploma of affiliation from the director of the Archconfraternity of St. Dizier, diocese of Langres (Haute-Marne), which is never refused, and which must be submitted to the ordinary before the inauguration of the Confraternity.

4. To hang in the church or chapel an image of the Sorrowful Face of our Lord *like the one in the oratory of M. Dupont,* and, if possible, to keep a lamp constantly burning before it.

5. To obtain a diploma of aggregation and *union of merits* and prayers from the director of the Confraternity at Tours, and in return assume the duty of propagating as zealously as possible the spirit of Reparation and devotion to the Holy

Face.

An Abridgment of Conditions for Membership.

1st. To be inscribed on the register of the Confraternity.

2nd. To obtain the Rules containing the Certificate of Admission.

3rd. Recite daily a Pater, Ave, Gloria, and the Act of Praise in a spirit of Reparation.

4th. Avoid blasphemies and the profanation of Sunday, and to at least repair those evils by an interior act of Reparation.

5th. Wear, at all times, the Cross of the Confraternity.

6th. To zealously propagate devotion to the Holy Face.

For further particulars apply to No. 134 Barrack Street, New Orleans, La., where these Rules of the Confraternity, the oil from the lamp of the Holy Face, scapulars, medals, pictures, photographs, crosses, books, chaplets, gospels of the Holy Name, and all else connected with the Reparation can be obtained. The oratories of the Holy Face are open to pilgrims and visitors daily from 5 A.M.to 6 P.M., where recommendations can be sent by mail or left by visitors. It is earnestly requested that persons who obtain graces should send a written account of the same and likewise have an ex-voto put up in thanksgiving for favors received through the Holy Face. These ex-votos can be procured on applying at the oratory. During Novenas lamps and candles will be kept burning when requested.

Promises Of Our Lord Jesus Christ in favor of all who Honor his Holy Face

1. They shall receive in themselves, by the impression of my Humanity, a bright irradiation from my Divinity, and shall be so illuminated by it in their inmost souls that by their likeness to my Face they shall shine with a brightness surpassing that of many others in eternal life. (St. Gertrude, book iv. ch. vii.)

2. St. Mechtilde having asked our Lord that those who celebrate the memory of his sweet Face should never be deprived of his amiable company, he replied: "Not one of them shall be separated from me." (St. Mechtilde, *De la Grace Spirituelle, book* i. ch. xiii.)

3. "Our Lord," said Sister Saint-Pierre, "has promised me that he will imprint his Divine likeness on the souls of those who honor his most Holy Countenance." (January 21, 1847.) "This Adorable Face is, as it were, the seal of the Divinity, which has the virtue of reproducing the likeness of God in the souls that are applied to it." (November 6, 1845.)

4. "By my Holy Face you shall work miracles." (October 27,

1845. Our Lord to Sister Marie de Saint-Pierre.)

5. "By my Holy Face you will obtain the conversion of many sinners. Nothing that you ask in making this offering will be refused to you. No one can know how pleasing the sight of my Face is to my Father!" (November 22, 1846.)

6. "As in a kingdom you can procure all you wish for with a coin marked with the prince's effigy, so in the kingdom of heaven you will obtain all you desire with the precious coin of my holy Humanity, which is my Adorable Countenance." (October 29, 1845.)

7. "All those who honor my Holy Face in a spirit of Reparation will by so doing perform the office of the pious Veronica." (October 27, 1S45.)

8. "According to the care you take in making Reparation to my Face, disfigured by blasphemies, so will I take care of yours, which has been disfigured by sin. I will reprint my image and render it as beautiful as it was on leaving the baptismal font." (Our Lord to Sister Marie de Saint-Pierre, November 3, 1845.)

9. "Our Lord has promised me," said again Sister Saint-Pierre, "for all those who defend his cause in this Work of Reparation, by words, by prayers, or in writing, that he will defend them before his Father; at their death he will purify their souls by effacing all the blots of sin and will restore to them their primitive beauty." (March 12, 1846.)

Prayers

Prayer of Pope Pius IX.

O my Jesus! cast upon us a look of mercy. Turn thy Face towards each of us, as thou didst to Veronica; not that we may see it with our bodily eyes, for this we do not deserve, but turn it towards our hearts, so that, remembering thee, we may ever draw from this fountain of strength the vigor necessary to sustain the combats of life. Amen.

(At an audience given to three Roman parishes, March 10, 1872. Several French bishops have attached indulgences to this prayer.)

Blessings of the High-Priest Aaron.

Benedicat tibi Dominus, et custodial te; Ostendat Dominus Faciem suam tibi, et misereatur tui.

The Lord bless thee and keep thee:

The Lord show his Face to thee and have mercy on thee. The Lord turn his Countenance to thee and give thee peace. (Numbers vi. 24-26.)

Aspirations.

Eternal Father, we offer thee the Adorable Face of thy well-beloved Son for the honor and glory of thy holy name and for the conversion of France and England. (Sister Marie de Saint-Pierre.)

May I die consumed by an ardent thirst to see the Face of our Lord and Saviour Jesus Christ. (Thought of St. Edmund, which M. Dupont frequently repeated towards the close of his life.)

(With approbation of the Archbishop of Tours, dated August 26, 1876.)

Devotion to the Holy Face of Our Lord

T he principal object of the devotion to the Holy Face is to offer respectful love and homage to the Adorable Face of Jesus disfigured in the Passion; to make reparation for blasphemy and the neglect of Holy Days, which outrages him afresh; and, lastly, to obtain of God the conversion of sinners and profaners of the Holy Day.

This touching devotion, which our Lord himself seems to have instituted on the day of his death by imprinting miraculously the traces of his bloodstained features on the Veil of Veronica, has always been known and practised in the Church. The holy Veil, carefully preserved at Home in the Vatican Basilica, receives many honors and marks of confidence. It is exposed several times a year to the veneration of the faithful. The Sovereign Pontiffs have accorded numerous indulgences to those who visit this signal relic with a pious intention. Many saints, men and women, have been distinguished by their devotion to the Divine Face, and have obtained all kinds of graces and blessings by invoking it. We will mention, among others, Saint Augustine, Saint Bernard, Saint. Gertrude, Saint Mechtilde, and in our own times, among those deceased in the odor of sanctity, Sister Marie de Saint-Pierre, Carmelite at Tours; Mother Marie-Therese, foundress of the *Congregation de l'Adoration Reparatrice;* lastly, the venerable M. Dupont, indefatigable propagator of the devotion to the Holy Face. Lately this devotion has become more general. It is an inspiration of the Holy Ghost passing through the Catholic world. It is a providential remedy offered to the world to combat the ravages of impiety and a shield against the scourges of divine justice.

The magnificent and consoling promises of our Lord, confirmed by a happy experience, show how pleasing the devotion of the Holy Face is to God and how useful to Christians. How many special graces, what unhoped-for conversions, what success in business, what supernatural lights have been obtained by this means! Above all, what a number of miraculous cures have been wrought by the virtue of the oil which burns constantly before the venerated picture at Tours!

It is remarkable that in no other part of his Adorable Body did our Lord suffer such outrages, such ignominies and insults, as in his amiable Face. No other circumstance of the Passion was as clearly announced by the prophets nor as minutely related by the Evangelists. All these details were not preserved in the Scriptures without a particular design of God. They exhort us to give a place among the mysteries of the sorrowful Passion of the Redeemer to the humiliations and sufferings of his most Holy Face. Christians who have at heart the glory of God and the salvation of others, honor with profound veneration the blood-stained and humiliated Face of your Saviour and pray to it with absolute confidence. In reparation of the impiety of the world offer to the Eternal Father this Adorable Face, with its sadness, its ignominy, its blood, its tears, its bruises, and its wounds. By so doing you will appease the anger of God, obtain the conversion of your erring brethren, contribute powerfully to the triumph of the Church and to the conversion of France and England and your own country, and you will participate in the glorious rewards promised by our Lord.

Pious Reflections Upon the Holy Face

(From the works of Sister Saint-Pierre)

1. *The Holy Face and the Holy Name of Jesus.*

A comparison, as simple as it is just, will show us how the impious by their blasphemy outrage the Adorable Face of our Lord, and how faithful souls glorify it by the praises they render to his Name and Person, Merit belongs to people, and the honor which they have is due to their name. When pronounced it carries with it merit or demerit, as it is deserved. The Holy Name of Jesus testifies to the glorious victory he has achieved over hell and expresses the adorable merits of his Person. The Holy Name of God testifies to his divinity and contains within itself all the perfections of the Creator; it follows, therefore, that those who blaspheme these sacred names directly attack God himself. Let us here recall those words of Jesus: "I belong to my Father, and my Father belongs to me." Jesus became passive through the Incarnation; it is he who suffers in his Adorable Face the outrages to the Name of God by blasphemy. There is a look of dumb pain upon the face of a man that is despised; his name and his face seem to bear an analogy one to the other. Behold a man, equally distinguished for his name and good qualities, in the presence of his enemies. They do not lift their hands to strike him, but they overwhelm him with abuse; they add derisive epithets to his name in place of the honorable titles which are his due. Observe, again, the look that passes over this man's face. Would you not think that all the abuse from the lips of his enemies is centered here, causing him to endure poignant anguish? The face is suffused with shame and vexation; the opprobrium and ignominy he suffers are harder to bear than real pain in other parts of his body. This, then, is a feeble explanation of our Lord's Face outraged by the blasphemy of the impious.

Represent to yourself this same man in the presence of his friends, who, hearing of the insults heaped upon him by his enemies, make haste to console him. They respect his dignity, do homage to his high name by giving him all the titles that belong to him. Do you not observe how this man's face changes under the sweet influence of this praise? There is a halo on his brow, which, spreading over the face, causes it to beam brightly; joy sparkles in his eye; there is a smile upon his lips—in a word, his faithful friends ha e healed the agonizing wounds of that face outraged by enemies; honor has superseded opprobrium. This is done by the friends of Jesus in the Work of Reparation; the glory with which they surround his Name beams upon his august brow and causes his Holy Face to rejoice.

2. Double motive for the Work of Reparation through the Holy Face.

This work has two ends, the Reparation of blasphemy and the Reparation of the profanation of Holy Days; it therefore embraces all outrages to God, and to his Holy Name.

Should the devotion of the Holy Face be united to this work? Yes, it forms part of its riches, and is its most precious ornament, since our Lord has made an offering of his Holy Face as an object of devotion to the members. They are all-powerful with God because of the offering they make him of that August and Divine Face, whose sight is so pleasing to him that it invariably softens, his anger and obtains for poor sinners his infinite mercy. Yes, when the Eternal Father contemplates the Face of his well-beloved Son, which has been buffeted, bruised, and covered with ignominy, the sight moves the bowels of his mercy. Let us endeavor to profit by this precious gift and let us beg this Divine Saviour to teach us the patience of his Face during the evil days.

3. Why the Holy Face is the Visible Sign of Reparation.

This August Face offered to our devotion is the ineffable mirror of the divine perfection contained and expressed in the Holy Name of God. As the Sacred Heart of Jesus is the visible sign offered to our devotion to typify the immensity of his love in the Sacrament of the Altar; in like manner the Adorable Face of our Lord is the visible sign offered to our devotion to repair the outrages committed by blasphemers towards the Majesty and Sovereignty of God, of which the Holy Face is the form, the mirror or expression. Thus, by virtue of this Holy Face offered to the Eternal Father we may appease his anger and obtain the conversion of the impious and blasphemous.

One may say with truth that sectarians and blasphemers renew towards the Holy Face of our Lord the opprobrium of the Passion. The impious who utter horrible language and blaspheme against the Holy Name of God, spitting in the Face of the Saviour and covering it with filth; and sectarians who attack the Church and religion renew the many blows the Face of our Lord has received, making this Divine Face sweat again with their efforts to efface his wonderful works. There is need of more Veronicas to do honor to this Divine Face, that has so few to adore it. All those who dedicate themselves to the Work of Reparation fill the place of the pious Israelite, and our Lord has constituted St. Louis, King of France, as one of the protectors of this

Work of Reparation, because of the zeal he showed for the glory of His Name.

4. The Office of the Pious Veronica.

The pious service rendered by St. Veronica to our Lord was that of wiping his Holy Face. Yes, all blasphemy hurled by the impious against the divinity they cannot reach falls, like the spittle of the Jews, on the Holy Face of our Lord, who has offered himself up as a victim for sinners. We thus see that by giving ourselves up to the exercise of repairing blasphemy, we render our Lord the same service as that of the pious Veronica, and that he looks upon those who offer it to him with the same beneficent eyes as those with which he looked upon that holy woman during the Passion.

5. Power of the Holy Face over St. Peter.

There are men on earth who can restore the body, but our Lord alone can restore the soul to the image of God; this, then, is the grace the Divine Master has promised to those who render to his Adorable Face the homage and honor it merits, with the intention to repair by this homage the opprobrium it receives from blasphemers.

One sees in the Apostle St. Peter an example of the power of the Holy Face. This apostle had by his sin effaced the image of God in his soul, but Jesus turned his Holy Face towards the unfaithful apostle and he became penitent: "Jesus looked upon Peter, and Peter wept bitterly." This Adorable Face is like the seal of the Divinity, with power to imprint in the souls of those who devote themselves to it the image of God.

6. The Holy Face represents the Adorable Trinity.

Remember, O my soul, the divine lesson thy heavenly Spouse has taught thee of the Adorable Face; remember that this Divine Head represents the Eternal Father, who is not begotten; that the Mouth of this Holy Face represents the Divine Word made Flesh by the Father, and the Eyes of this Holy and Silent Face represent the reciprocal love of the Father and the Son— for his Divine Eyes have but one light, one intelligence, and produce one only love, which is that of the Holy Ghost; behold in the Hair the diverse perfections of the Holy Trinity. Look upon the Majestic Head as a precious part of the Holy Humanity of our Lord, the image of the Unity of God; and it is this Adorable and Silent Face of the Saviour that blasphemers overwhelm with fresh insults. They thus renew in some measure the sufferings of the Passion in attacking by their blasphemy the Divinity of which it is the image.

Little Scapular of the Holy Face

The Scapular of the Holy Face is a little image of the Adorable Face, painted on linen, to be worn with devotion by pious souls as a testimony of their love towards our Lord, as a preservation against temptations and dangers of soul and body. It can be attached to the Scapular of our Lady of Mount Carmel, or to any other the person wears. There is no liturgical formality necessary for its reception, and the person who takes this Scapular contracts no other obligation than to wear it in the spirit of faith and reparation.

It is a little fac-simile of the Veil of St. Veronica, one of the greater relics of the Vatican Basilica in Pome.

Little Chaplet of the Holy Face.

The purpose of the Crown or Chaplet of the Holy Face is to honor the five Wounds pf our Lord Jesus Christ and to ask of God the triumph of his Holy Church.

This Chaplet is composed of a cross and thirty-nine beads; of these six are large beads and thirty-three small ones; to this Chaplet is attached a medal of the Holy Face. It would be well to recite it daily to obtain from God, by the Face of his well-beloved Son, the triumph of our holy mother, the Catholic Church. On the cross, which reminds us of the mystery of our Redemption, we begin the Chaplet by saying the words: *"Deus in adjutorium meum intende; Domine ad adjuvandum me festina"* ("Incline unto my aid, O God; O Lord, make haste to help me"), followed by the *Gloria Patri,* etc.

The thirty-three small beads represent the thirty-three years of the mortal life of our Divine Lord. The first thirty beads recall to us the thirty years of his hidden life, and are divided into five parts of six beads each, in honor of the five senses of touch, hearing, sight, smell, and taste of Jesus; and, as they were situated principally in his Holy Face, to make reparation for all the sufferings which our Lord has endured in his Face through each one of these senses.

The six beads are preceded by a large bead, followed by a *Gloria Patri,* etc., to recall the sense we wish to honor. The other beads mark the three years of the public life of our Lord and have for their intention to honor all the Wounds of his Adorable Face. These are also preceded by a large bead, to be followed by a *Gloria Patri,* etc., for the same intention.

On each large bead is said: "My Jesus, mercy" (100 days' indulgence). On the small beads is said: "Arise, O Lord, and let thy enemies be scattered, and let those that hate thee fly before thy Face."

The *Gloria Patri,* etc., is recited seven times in honor of the seven last words of Jesus upon the Gross and the seven Dolors of the Immaculate Virgin.

The Chaplet is concluded by saying on the medal: "God our protector, look down upon us and cast thine eyes upon the Face of thy

Christ." (With the approbation of N. J. Perehe, Archbishop of New Orleans.)

An Act of Resignation for the Sick

Thou didst speak, Lord Jesus, and the sins of the happy paralytic were forgiven ere thou hadst said, "Arise " (Mark ii. 2).

Knowing and believing firmly that thou hast given to thy priests the power of remitting sins, miserable sinner that I am, I will at once go to the tribunal of penance before imploring thee to cast the eyes of thine infinite mercy upon my bodily infirmities, and, submitting my heart and soul to thy holy will, O Lord, I will await in peace the accomplishment of my prayers on earth, with the hope of beholding, praising, and blessing thine Adorable Face in the eternity of heaven. Amen.

Formulas used by M. Dupont when anointing the sick with the oil of the Holy Face: "May the Lord deign to unite with us in making this unction and restore this sick person to health." In the name of the Father, etc. Or, "May the holy names of Jesus, Mary, and Joseph be known, blessed, and glorified throughout the entire world." Amen.

(Imprimatur: N. J. Perche, Archbishop of New Orleans.)

Collection of Prayers

The Act of Praise, or Golden Arrow.

May the most holy, most sacred, most adorable, most incomprehensible and ineffable Name of God be forever praised, blessed, loved, adored, and glorified in heaven and on earth by all the creatures of God, and by our Saviour Jesus Christ in the Most Holy Sacrament of the Altar. Amen.

(This act of praise in honor of the three Persons of the Holy Trinity is to be repeated three times.)

Prayer to the Eternal Father.

O All-Powerful and Eternal God, it is through the Heart of Jesus, thy Divine Son, my way, my truth, and my life, that I approach thee. I come through that Adorable Heart, in union with the holy angels and all the saints, to praise, bless, adore, and glorify thy Holy Name, scorned and blasphemed by so large a number of sinners. Accompanying in thought the good spirits, ministers of thy mercy, I make the circuit of the globe; seeking all souls redeemed by the blood of thy only Son, I offer them to thee by the hands of the Holy Virgin and glorious St. Joseph, under the protection of the angels and all the saints, supplicating thee, in the Name and through the merits of our Saviour Jesus, to convert all blasphemers and profaners of thy Holy Days, that we may have but one voice, one mind, and one heart to praise, bless, love, adore, and glorify thy Holy Name through the height, the depth, the breadth, the immensity, the fulness of honor of the praises and infinite adoration that the Sacred Heart of thy well-beloved Son accords thee—that Sacred Name which is the delight of the Holy Trinity.

Twenty-four Aspirations to Repair the Blasphemies that Occur During the 24 Hours of the Day

Twenty-four Aspirations to Repair the Blasphemies that Occur During the 24 Hours of the Day

(The Magnificat is said here.)

1. In union with the Sacred Heart of Jesus, come let us adore the admirable Name of God, which is above all names.

2. In union with the holy heart of Mary, come, etc.

3. In union with the glorious St. Joseph, come, etc.

4. In union with holy John the Baptist, come, etc.

5. In union with the choir of Seraphim, come, etc.

6. In union with the choir of Cherubim, come, etc.

7. In union with the choir of Thrones, come, etc.

8. In union with the choir of Dominations, come, etc.

9. In union with the choir of Virtues, come, etc.

10. In union with the choir of Powers, come, etc.

11. In union with the choir of Principalities, come, etc.

12. In union with the choir of Archangels, come, etc.

13. In union with the choir of Angels, come, etc.

14. In union with the Seven Spirits that are before the Throne of God, and the twenty-four elders, come, etc.

15. In union with the choir of Patriarchs, come, etc.

16. In union with the choir of Prophets, come, etc.

17. In union with the choir of the Apostles and the Four Evangelists, come etc.

18. In union with the choir of Martyrs, come, etc.

19. In union with the choir of the holy Pontiffs, come, etc.

20. In union with the choir of holy Confessors, come, etc.

21. In union with the choir of holy Virgins, come, etc.

22. In union with the choir of holy Women, come, etc.

23. In union with all the Celestial Courts, come, etc.

24. In union with all the Church and in the name of all men, come let us adore the admirable Name of God, and let us prostrate ourselves before him. Let us weep in the presence of God who made us, for he is the Lord our God; we are his people, and the sheep of his pasture.

Salutations to Our Lord Jesus Christ in Reparation of Blasphemy against his Sacred Person.

In union with the whole Church and the hearts of Mary and Joseph, all burning with love, and in the name of all men we salute, we adore, and we love thee, O Jesus of Nazareth, King of the Jews, full of sweetness and humility, of grace and truth. Mercy and justice belong to thee; love is thy substance; thou art the Christ, only Son of the living God, and the blessed fruit of the womb of the glorious Virgin Mary.

O Jesus, Good Shepherd, who didst give thy life for thy flock, by all thy holy wounds, thy divine tears, and thy precious sweat, by all the sighs, groans, pains, love, the merits of the thirty-three years of thy holy life contained within the ineffable sanctuary of thy loving Heart, take pity on us poor and miserable sinners. Convert all blasphemers and grant us a portion of thy divine merits now and at the hour of our death. *Amen.*

In this manner we must salute our Lord three times, to honor his divine life, his glorious life, and his mortal life.

Aspirations.

Eternal Father, I offer thee the body and blood of our Lord Jesus Christ in expiation of our sins and for the needs of thy Holy Church. Amiable Heart of Jesus, our mediator, appease thy Father and save sinners.

Powerful Heart of Mary, refuge of sinners, avert the shafts of divine justice.

St. Michael, pray for us.

St. Martin, pray for us.

St. Louis, pray for us.

O God our Protector, look upon us and cast thine eyes on the Face of thy Christ (Ps. lxxxviii. 9).

A Coronet to the Glory of the Holy Name of God for the Reparation of Blasphemy.

Instead of the "Credo" will be said:

We adore thee, O Jesus, and we bless thee, because by thy holy Cross thou hast redeemed the world.

On the three small beads of the cross say:

May the ever-Holy Name of God be glorified by the Holy Soul of the Word made flesh. May the ever-Holy Name of God be glorified by the Sacred Heart of the Incarnate Word. May the ever Adorable Name of God be glorified by all the wounds of the Incarnate Word.

On the three large beads say:

We invoke thee, O Sacred Name of the

living God, by the voice of Jesus in the Blessed Sacrament, and offer thee, by the blessed hands of Mary Immaculate, all the Sacred Hosts upon our altars as a sacrifice of reparation for all the blasphemies that outrage thy Holy Name.

On each of the ten small beads:

1. I salute thee, O Holy Name of the living God, through the Heart of Jesus in the Blessed Sacrament.

2. I venerate thee, O Holy Name of the living God, through the Heart of Jesus in the Blessed Sacrament.

3. I adore thee, O Holy Name of the living God, through the Heart of Jesus in the Blessed Sacrament.

4. I give thee glory, O Sacred Name of the living God, through the Heart of Jesus in the Blessed Sacrament.

5. I praise thee, O Sacred Name of the living God, through the Heart of Jesus in the Blessed Sacrament.

6. I admire thee, O Sacred Name of the living God, through the Heart of Jesus in the Blessed Sacrament.

7. I extol thee, O Sacred Name of the living God, through the Heart of Jesus in the Blessed Sacrament.

8. I magnify thee, O Sacred Name of the living God, through the Heart of Jesus in the Blessed Sacrament.

9. I love thee, O Sacred Name of the living God, through the Heart of Jesus in the Blessed Sacrament.

10. I bless thee, O Sacred Name of the living God, through the Heart of Jesus in the Blessed Sacrament.

Loving Aspirations to our Blessed Lord to Repair the Blasphemy of the Jews.

O Jesus, eternal truth and wisdom, who wast called a tempter and a madman, I adore thee and love thee with all my heart.

O Jesus, in whom dwelt all the riches of divine science, who wast looked upon as ignorant and as the son of a carpenter, I adore thee, etc.

O Jesus, source of life, who didst hear the Jews say of thee, "Will he kill himself?" because thou saidst, "I go where thou canst not follow me," I adore thee, etc.

O Jesus, Divine Word, who wast supposed to be possessed by a devil and wast called a Samaritan, I adore thee, etc.

O Jesus, God thrice holy, who wast treated as a sinner by the High-Priests, I adore thee, etc.

O Jesus, model of sobriety, whose enemies accused thee of gluttony, I adore thee, etc.

O Jesus, enemy of sin, but full of pity for the guilty, who wast called the friend of publicans and sinners, I adore thee, etc.

O Jesus, the splendor of the Father and the image of his substance, who wast accused of being a false prophet, I adore thee, etc.

O Jesus, the enemy of falsehood, who didst hear the Jews cast doubts on thy words by saying with irony, "Thou art not yet fifty and hast seen Abraham?" I adore thee, etc.

O Jesus, all-powerful God, who, to conform with our nature, which thou hadst taken upon thyself, wished to hide and go from the Temple, that thou mightest not be stoned by thine enemies, I adore thee, etc.

O Jesus, only Son and faithful worshipper of the living God, who wast accused by the High-Priest of blasphemy and wast adjudged worthy of death, I adore thee, etc.

O Jesus, King of glory, who, full of sweetness and humility, didst permit thy Face to be spit upon, thy Head to be covered with a veil and beaten and bruised, I adore thee, etc.

O Jesus, who dost fathom our hearts and loins, to whom nothing is hidden, and who didst suffer without complaint these insolent words, "If thou art the Christ, tell who has struck thee," I adore thee, etc.

O Jesus, King of peace, accused of perverting the nation and preventing the payment of the tribute-money, of causing the people to revolt and calling thyself King and Messiah, I adore thee, etc.

O Jesus, King of kings, scorned by Herod and his court, and dressed in derision in a white robe like a madman, I adore thee, etc.

O Jesus, full of love, who didst hear the cry of the people, "Let this one die, and restore Barabbas to us," "Let his blood be upon us and upon our children," I adore thee, etc.

O Jesus, King of heaven and earth, crowned with thorns, shamefully beaten, and so cruelly outraged by these words, "We salute thee, O King of the Jews," I adore thee, etc.

O Jesus, of infinite bounty, principle of all being, Sovereign Master of the world, who didst hear these words of doom, "Crucify him, crucify him! lead him away! lead him away! We have no other king but Caesar," I adore thee, etc.

O Jesus, worthy of all praise, who when upon the Cross wast blasphemed by the passers-by, the impenitent thief, the High-Priests, the elders of the people, and the scribes and soldiers, I adore thee, etc.

O Jesus, holy victim of sinners, who didst hear thine enemies say to thee, "He saved others and cannot save himself; let this Christ, this King of Israel, now come down from the Cross, that we may see and believe in him," I adore thee, etc.

O Jesus, full of confidence, love, and respect for thy Divine Father, who wast wounded with the most lively pain when they said on seeing thee die, "He puts his trust in God; if God love him let him deliver him now, for he has said, I am the Son of God," I adore thee, and I love thee with all my heart.

Prayer.

I bitterly compassionate, O my Saviour, Jesus Christ, the anguish endured by thy divine Heart when thou didst hear blasphemies that thine enemies poured forth against thee and thy heavenly Father; but what, O Jesus, must be thy sorrow in seeing that after thou hast given thy life, and the last drop of thy blood, for the salvation of men, thou shouldst still have, after the lapse of centuries, new enemies who reiterate a thousand times these blasphemies! Accept, my sweet Jesus, the ardent desire we have to repair all the outrages and scorn thou hast received, and still dost receive every day, from heretics and the impious. Oh! why cannot we protect thee from the anger of those that hate thee, and who are leagued against thee and thy Holy Church, thy stainless spouse? Repeat with us, O merciful Jesus, that touching prayer thou didst offer to thy Divine Father before breathing thy last sigh: "Forgive them, Father, for they know not what they do!" We offer thee, as reparation for the many offences against thee, all the glory, honor, and praise, and all the joy, that the Holy Virgin and St. Joseph, the Saints and elect, did give thee and will ever give thee in time and eternity. *Amen.*

Coronet

In honor of the Holy Name of Jesus, for the reparation of the blasphemies and injuries inflicted by the Jews when they crowned Him with thorns.

I salute thee, Word of God, Saviour of men; I adore thee, Sacred Host, true and living flesh, perfect divinity, true God and true man. O Jesus, who gavest me my life, I adore thee and I love thee with all my heart.

On the three small beads of the cross say:

We give thee glory, O Jesus, and we invoke thy Holy Name.

On the five large beads say:

The *Gloria Patri,* one *Pater,* and one *Ave.*

On each of the ten small beads say:

1. May the Holy Name of Jesus be blessed!

2. May the Holy Name of Jesus be our meditation!

3. May the Holy Name of Jesus fill us with wonder!

4. May the Holy Name of Jesus be glorified!

5. May the Holy Name of Jesus be loved!

6. May the Holy Name of Jesus be crowned with honor!

7. May the Holy Name of Jesus be exalted!

8. May the Holy Name of Jesus be reverenced!

9. May the Holy Name of Jesus be invoked!

10. May the Holy Name of Jesus be praised and blessed in time and in eternity!

Prayer to our Lord Jesus Christ, the True Repairer of Outrages committed against the Glory of his Father.

O Jesus, at the sight of the blasphemers of the Holy Name of God we pray thee to renew with us the prayer thou didst address to thy Divine Father, which has been transmitted to us by St. John, thy beloved disciple: "My Father, glorify thy Name!" In that hour came a voice from heaven saying these words: "I have already glorified it and shall glorify it yet more!" May this Voice be heard on earth; we beg it of thee by thy sacred wounds and Adorable Face. As to ourselves, we will not cease to supplicate thee in thine own words: "Our Father who art in heaven, hallowed be thy Name. Thy kingdom come, thy will be done on earth as it is in heaven."

Litany of the Holy Face

In Reparation for Blasphemies, and to implore of God, by the Adorable Face of his Son, the conversion of blasphemers.

Lord, *have mercy on us.*

Jesus Christ, *have mercy on us.*

Lord, *have mercy on us.*

Jesus Christ, *hear us.*

Jesus Christ, *graciously hear us.*

Holy Virgin Mary, *pray for us.*

O Adorable Face, adored with profound respect by Mary and Joseph when they saw thee for the first time; *have mercy on us. Gloria Patri.*

O Adorable Face, which in the stable of Bethlehem didst ravish with joy the Angels, the shepherds, and the wise men,

O Adorable Face, which in the Temple didst transpierce with a dart of love the saintly Simeon and the prophetess Anna,

O Adorable Face, which wast bathed in tears in thy holy infancy,

O Adorable Face, which, appearing in the Temple, didst fill with admiration the Doctors of the Law,]

O Adorable Face, whose charms were so ravishing, and whose grace was so attractive,

O Adorable Face, whose nobility characterized every feature,

O Adorable Face, contemplated by the Angels,

O Adorable Face, sweet delight of the Saints,

O Adorable Face, masterpiece of the Holy Ghost, in which the Eternal Father is well pleased,

O Adorable Face, delight of Mary and Joseph,

O Adorable Face, ineffable mirror of the divine perfections,

O Adorable Face, which appeasest the anger of God,

O Adorable Face, which makest the devils tremble,

O Adorable Face, treasure of grace and blessings,

O Adorable Face, exposed in the desert to the inclemencies of the weather,

O Adorable Face, which wast bathed with sweat in thy journeys and scorched with the heat and sun,

O Adorable Face, whose expression was all divine,

O Adorable Face, whose modesty and meekness attracted both just and sinners,

O Adorable Face, troubled and weeping at the tomb of Lazarus,

O Adorable Face, brilliant as the sun and radiant with glory on Mount Thabor,

O Adorable Face, sorrowful at the sight of Jerusalem and shedding tears over that ungrateful city,

O Adorable Face, bowed to the earth in the Garden of Olives and covered with confusion for our sins,

O Adorable Face, bathed in a bloody sweat,

O Adorable Face, kissed by the traitor Judas,

O Adorable Face, whose sanctity and majesty struck the soldiers with fear and cast them to the ground,

O Adorable Face, struck by an infamous servant, blindfolded, and profaned by the sacrilegious hands of thine enemies,

O Adorable Face, defiled with spittle and bruised by so many buffets and blows,

O Adorable Face, whose divine look wounded the heart of Peter with repentant sorrow and love,

O Adorable Face, humbled for us at the tribunals of Jerusalem,

O Adorable Face, which didst preserve thy serenity when Pilate pronounced the fatal sentence,

O Adorable Face, covered with sweat and blood, and falling into the mire under the weight of the cross,

O Adorable Face, wiped with a veil by a pious woman on the road to Calvary,

O Adorable Face, raised on the instrument of the most shameful punishment;

O Adorable Face, whose incomparable beauty was obscured under the fearful cloud of the sins of the world,

O Adorable Face, covered with the sad shades of death,

O Adorable Face, washed and anointed by Mary and the holy women, and covered with a shroud,

O Adorable Face, enclosed in the sepulcher,

O Adorable Face, all resplendent with glory and beauty on the day of the resurrection,

O Adorable Face, all dazzling with light at the moment of thy ascension,

O Adorable Face, hidden in the Eucharist.

O Adorable Face, which wilt appear at the end of time in the clouds, with great power and majesty, *Have mercy on us. Gloria.*

O Adorable Face, which wilt cause sinners to tremble, *Have mercy on us. Gloria.*

O Adorable Face, which wilt fill the just with joy for all eternity, *Have mercy on us. Gloria.*

Lamb of God, who takest away the sins of the world, *Spare us, O Lord.*

Lamb of God, who takest away the sins of the world, *Graciously hear us, O Lord.*

Lamb of God, who takest away the sins of the world, *Have mercy on us, O Lord.*

Prayer.

I salute, adore, and love thee, O Jesus, my Saviour, covered anew with outrages by blasphemers, and I offer thee, through the heart of thy Blessed Mother, the worship of all the angels and saints, as an incense and a perfume of sweet odor, most humbly beseeching thee, by the virtue of thy Sacred Face, to repair and renew in me and in all men thine image disfigured by sin. *Amen.*

Pater, Ave, Gloria.

Another Prayer.

I salute, adore, and love thee, O Adorable Face of Jesus my Beloved, noble image of the Divinity; with all the powers of my soul I apply myself to thee, and pray thee most humbly to imprint in us all the features of thy divine likeness. *Amen.*

By a Rescript dated 27th of January 1853, His Holiness Pope Pius IX grants to all who recite with a contrite heart these prayers in honor of the Holy Face of Jesus Christ an indulgence of a hundred days for each time, applicable to the souls in Purgatory.

Act of Reparation
for blasphemy and irreverence, to be recited at the monthly meeting of the Confraternity.

O God, infinitely worthy of all adoration and love, I prostrate myself at thy feet, filled with grief for the blasphemies uttered against thy Holy Name, and for the offences committed against thy divine worship and the observances of thy Church.

O my God, this blasphemy is the profanation of that which is most holy in the height of thine inaccessible sanctuary; it is an attack upon thine infinite majesty; an outrage against the Face of thy Divine Son; a crime without excuse, without any other motive than that wickedness which hates thee, O God, infinitely worthy of all love!

We beg pardon, O Lord, a thousand times pardon, for these blasphemies. Would that we could prevent them by the sacrifice of all that we are or that we possess! At least it is in the sincerity of our hearts that we desire with all our power to combat this horrible crime, and for all we hear or know to offer instantly, by the merits of the Face of thy Christ, our humble and sorrowful expiation.

But that which is most grievous to us is that, while blasphemy and infidelity daily increase, the adoration due to thee diminishes. Alas, now, even more than in the days of the prophet Ezechiel, men neglect and profane thy holy days, because their hearts are given to idols. Slaves of avarice and of pleasure, they have no longer time for thy worship nor attraction to thine altars. The days set apart for thy service are profaned by their worldliness or pleasure. They abandon thine house; they fly from the preaching of thy word; they despise the sacraments and graces of the sanctuary to give themselves to labors forbidden or to amusements still more criminal.

O Lord, grant us the grace to make reparation for this contempt and forgetfulness of thee by the zeal and fervor of our adoration. Bless this Confraternity established under the invocation of the Adorable Face of Jesus Christ, that by its prayers and sacrifices it may bring back to thy worship and to the observances of thy Church the unfaithful who have strayed from thee. Receive our vows and promises never to transgress thy sacred precepts, neither in our own persons nor by those who are under our charge; and, in every way possible to us, to procure the obedience and honor which are due to thee.

May the most Adorable Name of the Lord be glorified forever!

May the holy days of thy Church be sanctified by all men! Amen. Amen.

Saint Michael, *Pray for us.*

Saint Peter, *Pray for us.*

Saint Martin, *Pray for us.*

Saint Louis, *Pray for us.*

Saint Veronica, *Pray for us.*

O God, our protector, look upon the Face of thy Christ, and we shall be saved!

An Offering

of the Infinite Merits of our lord Jesus Christ to his

Eternal Father in order to appease the divine justice and draw mercy on France.

Eternal Father, turn thine offended eyes from culpable France, whose face has become hideous in thy eyes, and look upon the Face of thy Son which we offer thee— this well-beloved Son, in whom thou art well pleased. Listen, we beseech thee, to the voice of his Blood and his wounds, which cry out for mercy.

Eternal Father, behold the Incarnation of Jesus, thy Divine Son, and his sojourn in the womb of his Blessed Mother. We offer this to thee for the honor and glory of thy Holy Name and for the salvation of France.

Eternal Father, behold the birth of Jesus in the stable of Bethlehem and the mysteries of his most holy infancy. We offer them to thee, etc.

Eternal Father, behold the poor, hidden, and laborious life of Jesus at Nazareth. We offer it to thee, etc.

Eternal Father, behold the baptism of Jesus and his forty days' retreat in the desert. We offer these to thee, etc.

Eternal Father, behold the journeys, the vigils, the prayers, miracles, and sermons of Jesus. We offer them to thee, etc.

Eternal Father, behold the Last Supper which Jesus made with his disciples, at which he washed their feet and instituted the august sacrament of the Eucharist. We offer this to thee, etc.

Eternal Father, behold the agony of Jesus in the Garden of Olives, the sweat of blood which covered his Body and flowed to the ground. We offer this to thee, etc.

Eternal Father, behold the outrages which Jesus received before his judges, and his condemnation to death. We offer them to thee, etc.

Eternal Father, behold Jesus burdened with his cross and walking towards the place where he is to be immolated. We offer him to thee, etc.

Eternal Father, behold Jesus crucified between two thieves, tasting gall and vinegar, blasphemed by the Jews, and dying to repair thy glory and to save the world. We offer him to thee, etc.

Eternal Father, behold the Sacred Head of Jesus crowned with thorns. We offer it to thee, etc.

Eternal Father, behold the Adorable Face of Jesus bruised with buffets, covered with sweat, dust, and blood. We offer it to thee, etc.

Eternal Father, behold the Adorable Body of Jesus taken down from the cross. We offer it to thee, etc.

Eternal Father, behold the heart, soul, and divinity of Jesus, this holy Victim who in dying has triumphed over sin. We offer them to thee, etc.

Eternal Father, behold all that Jesus Christ, thy only Son, has done during the thirty-three years of his mortal life to accomplish the work of our Redemption. Behold all the mysteries of his holy life. We offer them to thee, etc.

Eternal Father, behold all the desires, all the thoughts, words, actions, virtues, perfections, and prayers, of Jesus Christ; also all his sufferings and humiliations. We offer them to thee, etc.

Eternal Father, behold the crib, the swaddling-bands which have served Jesus at his birth. We offer them to thee, etc.

Eternal Father, behold the cross, the nails, the crown of thorns, the reed, the bloody scourge, the column, the lance, the sepulcher, the winding-sheet, and all the instruments which were used in the Passion of Jesus, thy Divine Son. We offer them to thee, etc.

A Hundred Offerings
of our Lord Jesus Christ to His Eternal Father.

Thirty-three Offerings of Jesus Christ in his Infancy and Hidden Life.

1. Eternal Father, I offer thee Jesus, Incarnate in the womb of the Virgin Mary for the salvation of men.

2. Eternal Father, I offer thee Jesus, sanctifying St. John the Baptist in the womb of his mother, St. Elizabeth.

3. Eternal Father, I offer thee Jesus, a captive for nine months in the chaste womb of his Blessed Mother.

4. Eternal Father, I offer thee Jesus, rejected by the inhabitants of Bethlehem.

5. Eternal Father, I offer thee Jesus, coming forth from the womb of his Mother and born in a poor stable.

6. Eternal Father, I offer thee Jesus, wrapped in swaddling-clothes and laid in a manger.

7. Eternal Father, I offer thee Jesus, trembling with cold and warmed by the breath of an ox and an ass.

8. Eternal Father, I offer thee Jesus, weeping for our sins in the manger.

9. Eternal Father, I offer thee Jesus, by the hands of Mary and St. Joseph, for the salvation of the world.

10. Eternal Father, I offer thee Jesus, nursed by Mary.

11. Eternal Father, I offer thee Jesus, adored by angels in the

stable of Bethlehem.

12. Eternal Father, I offer thee Jesus, adored by the poor shepherds.

13. Eternal Father, I offer thee Jesus, circumcised and named Jesus, beginning to fulfil the office of Saviour in offering thee the first-fruits of his Blood.

14. Eternal Father, I offer thee Jesus, receiving the gifts and adorations of the Magi.

15. Eternal Father, I offer thee all the glory that Jesus has rendered thee during the forty days he dwelt in the stable of Bethlehem.

16. Eternal Father, I offer thee Jesus, brought to the Temple by Mary and Joseph, and received with great joy by the holy old man Simeon and the prophetess Anna.

17. Eternal Father, I offer thee Jesus, who offers himself to thy divine justice to be the repairer of thy outraged glory and the holy victim of sinners.

18. Eternal Father, I offer thee Jesus, fleeing into Egypt to avoid the murderous hand of Herod.

19. Eternal Father, I offer thee Jesus, poor and unknown in his exile, but tenderly loved and profoundly adored by Mary, Joseph, and the Angels.

20. Eternal Father, I offer thee Jesus, carried in the arms of Mary and Joseph and submitting to all the trials of infancy.

21. Eternal Father, I offer thee Jesus, nursed by his Divine Mother for fifteen months.

22. Eternal Father, I offer thee the first steps, the first words, the first actions of thy Divine Son Jesus.

23. Eternal Father, I offer thee all that Jesus suffered in the seven years of his exile in Egypt.

24. Eternal Father, I offer thee Jesus, returning to Nazareth between Mary and Joseph.

25. Eternal Father, I offer thee Jesus, growing in age and in wisdom before God and men.

26. Eternal Father, I offer thee Jesus, conducted to the Temple at the age of twelve years to celebrate the Passover.

27. Eternal Father, I offer thee Jesus, remaining three days in the Temple in the midst of the Doctors of the Law, and filling them with admiration.

28. Eternal Father, I offer thee Jesus, found by Mary and Joseph, returning to Nazareth, and being perfectly submissive to them.

29. Eternal Father, I offer thee Jesus, hiding his glory in the workshop of St. Joseph, and seeming to be only a carpenter.

30. Eternal Father, I offer thee Jesus, working for his support by the sweat of his brow.

31. Eternal Father, I offer thee Jesus, assisting St. Joseph during his last illness and at the hour of his death.

32. Eternal Father, I offer thee Jesus, consoling Mary, his Blessed Mother, for the death of her holy spouse.

33. Eternal Father, I offer thee all the glory that Jesus has rendered thee during the thirty-three years of his hidden and laborious life, also all the merits he has acquired for us.

Eternal Father, I offer thee all the glory that our Divine Saviour Jesus has rendered thee during the thirty years of his hidden and laborious life, and all the merits he has acquired for us from the moment of his Divine Incarnation until his evangelical Life. I make this offering for the honor and glory of thy Holy Name, in reparation for the indignities offered our Saviour; finally, for the wants of the Holy Church, the salvation of France, and the Work of Reparation.

Thirty-three Offerings of Jesus in his Evangelical Life.

1. Eternal Father, I offer thee Jesus, baptized in the river Jordan by St. John the Baptist.

2. Eternal Father, I offer thee Jesus, led by the spirit into the desert, and suffering there hunger and thirst.

3. Eternal Father, I offer thee Jesus, spending his nights in the desert among wild beasts.

4. Eternal Father, I offer thee Jesus, passing days and nights in prayer, watering the ground with his divine tears, in expiation for our sins.

5. Eternal Father, I offer thee Jesus, tempted by the evil spirit to change stones into bread.

6. Eternal Father, I offer thee Jesus, carried by Satan to the top of the Temple, and tempted by this evil spirit to cast himself

down.

7. Eternal Father, I offer thee Jesus, carried by Satan to the top of a high mountain with the promise of all the kingdoms of the world.

8. Eternal Father, I offer thee Jesus, triumphing over the temptations of the evil spirit and confronting him with the words of Holy Scripture.

9. Eternal Father, I offer thee Jesus, in the desert taking the food ministered by the Angels.

10. Eternal Father, I offer thee all the glory that Jesus has rendered thee in the desert and all the merits he has acquired for us.

11. Eternal Father, I offer thee Jesus, coming forth from the desert and going to make known to his Blessed Mother the mission he was about to commence.

12. Eternal Father, I offer thee Jesus, choosing poor fishermen for his Apostles.

13. Eternal Father, I offer thee Jesus, going from city to city, from town to town, preaching everywhere the Kingdom of God, and making known his Divine Father.

14. Eternal Father, I offer thee Jesus, followed by immense crowds even to the deserts.

15. Eternal Father, I offer thee Jesus, multiplying the loaves and fishes to feed the multitude.

16. Eternal Father, I offer thee Jesus, consoling the afflicted.

17. Eternal Father, I offer thee Jesus, curing the sick and raising the dead.

18. Eternal Father, I offer thee Jesus, driving out the evil spirit from those who were possessed.

19. Eternal Father, I offer thee Jesus, giving sight to the blind and hearing to the deaf.

20. Eternal Father, I offer thee Jesus, curing the lame and making the dumb to speak.

21. Eternal Father, I offer thee Jesus, converting sinners and doing good to all.

22. Eternal Father, I offer thee Jesus, weeping for the death of Lazarus and raising him to life.

23. Eternal Father, I offer thee Jesus, converting Mary Magdalen.

24. Eternal Father, I offer thee Jesus, weary by the wayside and seated on Jacob's Well.

25. Eternal Father, I offer thee Jesus, asking drink of the Samaritan woman, converting her, and making known to her that he was the promised Messias.

26. Eternal Father, I offer thee Jesus, confounding his enemies with an admirable wisdom when they presented before him a woman taken in adultery.

27. Eternal Father, I offer thee Jesus, driving the sellers out of the

Temple.

28. Eternal Father, I offer thee Jesus, transfigured on Mt. Thabor, conversing with Moses and Elias on the greatness of the sorrows of his Passion.

29. Eternal Father, I offer thee Jesus, embracing and blessing little children, bidding us to become as one of them to enter the Kingdom of Heaven.

30. Eternal Father, I offer thee Jesus, entering the city of Jerusalem in triumph, and received as a King by the people.

31. Eternal Father, I offer thee Jesus, weeping for the sins of Jerusalem.

32. Eternal Father, I offer thee Jesus alone and abandoned, obliged on the evening of the Feast to seek the hospitality of Martha and Mary, at Bethany.

33. Eternal Father, I offer thee all the glory that Jesus has rendered thee during the three years of his divine preachings.

Eternal Father, I offer thee all the glory that Jesus, our Divine Saviour, has rendered thee, all the infinite merits he has acquired for us from the moment of his evangelical life until his Passion.

I make this offering for the honor and glory of thy Holy Name, to repair the outrages offered our Divine Saviour; finally, for the wants of the Holy Church, the salvation of France, and the extension of the Work of Reparation.

Thirty-four Offerings of Jesus in his Suffering and Glorious Life.

1. Eternal Father, I offer thee Jesus, sold for thirty pieces of silver by the traitor Judas.

2. Eternal Father, I offer thee Jesus, taking his Last Supper with his Apostles.

3. Eternal Father, I offer thee Jesus, humbling himself unto washing the feet of his Apostles.

4. Eternal Father, I offer thee Jesus, instituting the Adorable Sacrament of the Eucharist and ordaining his Apostles priests of the New Law.

5. Eternal Father, I offer thee Jesus, praying and in an agony in the Garden of Olives.

6. Eternal Father, I offer thee Jesus, suffering in his Divine Heart all the sorrows of his Passion and watering the earth with a profuse sweat of blood.

7. Eternal Father, I offer thee Jesus, sorrowful unto death in the Garden of Olives, burdened with all the sins of the world, and accepting the chalice from thy Hand.

8. Eternal Father, I offer thee Jesus, betrayed and kissed by the perfidious Judas, delivering himself up to his enemies to be bound and blindfolded for our sins.

9. Eternal Father, I offer thee Jesus, abandoned by his disciples, maltreated and outraged by the soldiers, and led to the house of the high-priest Annas.

10. Eternal Father, I offer thee Jesus, interrogated and receiving a blow from a servant.

11. Eternal Father, I offer thee Jesus, conducted to the house of

Caiphas and accused by false witnesses.

12. Eternal Father, I offer thee Jesus, treated as a blasphemer because he declared to his enemies that he was the Son of God.

13. Eternal Father, I offer thee Jesus, despised, struck, and spit upon during that horrible night, and treated as the vilest slave.

14. Eternal Father, I offer thee Jesus, conducted in chains to Pilate's house.

15. Eternal Father, I offer thee Jesus, led to the court of Herod and despised by that impious king.

16. Eternal Father, I offer thee Jesus, reconducted to the house of Pilate, treated with contempt and humiliations on the streets of Jerusalem by a nation which he had overwhelmed with benefits.

17. Eternal Father, I offer thee Jesus, tied to the column and torn by the stripes of the scourge.

18. Eternal Father, I offer thee Jesus, covered with wounds and blood, trampled upon by his executioners.

19. Eternal Father, I offer thee Jesus, arrayed as a mock-king, crowned with thorns, robed in a scarlet mantle, his arms tied, and a reed for a scepter in his Hand.

20. Eternal Father, I offer thee Jesus, outraged, despised, and then shown to the people.

21. Eternal Father, I offer thee Jesus, rejected by his people, who with loud voices demanded his death and preferred to him an infamous thief, Barabbas.

22. Eternal Father, I offer thee Jesus, condemned by Pilate to the death of the cross.

23. Eternal Father, I offer thee Jesus, given over to an insolent multitude, who vent upon this sweet Lamb, so meek and humble of heart, all that the darkest malice could devise.

24. Eternal Father, I offer thee Jesus, going forth from Pilate's hall between the two thieves, carrying the cross upon his Divine Shoulders, bruised and bleeding.

25. Eternal Father, I offer thee Jesus, exhausted by fatigue, falling several times under the heavy burden of his cross, beaten and overwhelmed with injurious treatment by his executioners.

26. Eternal Father, I offer thee Jesus, on the summit of Calvary, despoiled of his garments and extending himself on the tree of the cross as a Lamb without stain.

27. Eternal Father, I offer thee Jesus, nailed with heavy blows of the hammer to the cross.

28. Eternal Father, I offer thee Jesus, suspended for three hours between heaven and earth, satiated with revilings, partaking of gall and vinegar, and tasting with delight the intensity of interior and exterior sufferings.

29. Eternal Father, I offer thee Jesus, asking forgiveness for his executioners, granting pardon to the good thief, and giving

us his most Blessed Mother.

30. Eternal Father, I offer thee Jesus, consummating his sacrifice and yielding up his Holy Soul into thy Hands, uttering a loud cry to call all sinners to him, inclining his Head to give them the kiss of peace and the last sigh of his Heart.

31. Eternal Father, I offer thee Jesus, his Heart pierced by a lance, his Sacred Body covered with wounds and blood, taken down from the cross and placed in the arms of his Divine Mother.

32. Eternal Father, I offer thee Jesus, embalmed and shrouded by his Holy Mother, assisted by his faithful friends; then carried to the sepulcher and remaining therein three days, as he had foretold.

33. Eternal Father, I offer thee Jesus, rising victorious from the tomb and visiting his Blessed Mother.

34. Eternal Father, I offer thee Jesus, appearing to his Apostles and the holy women for their consolation and instruction, gloriously ascending to Heaven in their presence forty days after his Resurrection.

Eternal Father, I offer thee all the glory that Jesus Christ, our Divine Saviour, has rendered thee, as well as all the merits he has acquired for us during his sorrowful and glorious life. I make this offering for the honor and glory of thy Holy Name, in reparation for the indignities offered to our Saviour—in fine, for the needs of the Holy Church, for the salvation of France and the entire world, and for the extension of the Work of Reparation.

This is my well-beloved Son, in whom I am well pleased. Hear ye him.
In truth I say to thee that all thou wilt ask the Father in my Fame he will
grant. Ask, and thou shalt receive.

The Sacred Humanity of Jesus,

And the holy use he made of his Senses, offered to the Eternal Father to
repair and efface the sins we have committed by ours.

Eternal Father, I offer thee the Sacred Feet of Jesus, walking and travelling, and finally pierced by rough nails, to repair our criminal steps.

Eternal Father, I offer thee all the devout and respectful prostrations of Jesus before thy Divine Majesty, to repair all our irreverences in thy holy presence.

Eternal Father, I offer thee the Divine Hands of Jesus, which accomplished so many good works, and nevertheless were pierced by rough nails, to repair all the sins of our wicked hands and our iniquitous works.

Eternal Father, I offer thee the Divine Arms of Jesus, fatigued by labor and torn by the whips of his executioners, to atone for our sins of sloth and all our other crimes.

Eternal Father, I offer thee the Divine Head of Jesus, crowned with thorns, his hair covered with blood, to atone for our sins of pride and all our criminal thoughts.

Eternal Father, I offer thee the Adorable Eyes and looks of Jesus, full of sweetness and majesty, to atone for our sins of immodesty and curiosity.

Eternal Father, I offer thee also his sleep, his vigils, his tears which flowed from his Divine Eyes, to merit the pardon of our faults.

Eternal Father, I offer thee the mortification of the smell of Jesus, to atone for all the sins of sensuality of which we are guilty.

Eternal Father, I offer thee the Adorable Mouth of Jesus, his divine words, and his admirable silence, to repair all the sins that our bad and unruly tongue has committed. I offer thee also his fasts and his frugal meals, to repair all our sins of gluttony and intemperance.

Eternal Father, I offer thee the Adorable Face of Jesus, covered with spittle, sweat, dust, and blood, bruised by buffets, and his beard torn out, to repair the pride and vanity, also all the other sins, of worldlings.

Eternal Father, I offer thee the prayers, praises, and thanksgivings of Jesus, to repair blasphemies and all sins committed against the glory of thy Name.

Eternal Father, I offer thee the Sacred Body of Jesus, covered with wounds, to repair all the sins of our corrupt flesh. We offer thee the seven effusions of his precious Blood, to purify us from our crimes.

Eternal Father, I offer thee the inflamed Heart of Jesus, pierced by a lance, to repair all the sins committed by our hearts. I offer also all the desires, sighs, thoughts, affections, prayers, and virtues, all the adorable perfections of this Divine Heart, to cover the poverty of our poor, miserable hearts.

Eternal Father, I offer thee the holy Soul of Jesus, that sacrificed itself for us and gave itself into thy hands at the moment of death. By the glory and merits of this most holy Soul, we pray thee to pardon and justify our criminal souls.

Eternal Father, I offer thee the divine, glorious, and laborious life of Jesus. We beseech thee, by the holiness of his interior life, to pardon our lives, spent in indifference and dissipation.

Eternal Father, I offer thee the eternal birth of Jesus in the splendor of thy glory; I offer also all the praises, honor, and eternal love he has for thee, to repair all the impieties and blasphemies of poor blinded sinners.

Eternal Father, I offer thee this Divine Jesus, to adore, love, and glorify in him and by him all thy adorable perfections and thy Sacred Name, which is unknown to creatures, but which expresses all that thou art, and which thy Divine Son Jesus alone knows and adores in spirit and in truth, in the name of all souls redeemed by his precious Blood.

I salute, adore, and love thee, O God the Father and God the Son, in the ineffable embraces of thy Divinity. I embrace with affection in the Sacred Heart of Jesus all creatures of heaven and earth, and I kiss thee with the eternal kiss of the Holy Ghost.

God has so loved the world that he has given his only-begotten Son to be its Redeemer.

An Offering

To the Eternal Father of the Things which his Adorable Son used during his Mortal Life— Precious Relics of Jesus.

Eternal Father, I offer thee the manger and hay upon which Jesus was laid at his birth. I offer also his poor swaddling-clothes and bands.

Eternal Father, I offer thee the two little doves and five pieces of silver given by the Blessed Virgin and St. Joseph to redeem Jesus at his Presentation.

Eternal Father, I offer thee the tunic which Mary wove for the Infant Jesus.

Eternal Father, I offer thee the cup from which the Infant Jesus drank.

Eternal Father, I offer thee the hammer, axe, saw, and other tools which the Divine Carpenter Jesus used.

Eternal Father, I offer thee all the work he made.

Eternal Father, I offer thee the scourge which Jesus made with his Divine Hands to drive the sellers from the Temple.

Eternal Father, I offer thee the four didrachmas which Jesus made St. Peter take from the fish's mouth to pay the tribute.

Eternal Father, I offer thee the basin in which Jesus washed the feet of his Apostles, and the linen with which he was girded.

Eternal Father, I offer thee the chalice which Jesus held in his Divine Hands after the Supper when he changed the wine into his precious Blood.

Eternal Father, I offer thee the thirty pieces of silver with which the Jews bought Jesus.

Eternal Father, I offer thee the cords that bound Jesus in the Garden of Olives.

Eternal Father, I offer thee the iron gauntlet from which Jesus received a buffet.

Eternal Father, I offer thee the band with which the Jews blindfolded the eyes of Jesus.

Eternal Father, I offer thee the gag which Jesus' enemies thrust into his mouth.

Eternal Father, I offer thee all the instruments which were used to torment our Lord during the night of his bitter Passion.

Eternal Father, I offer thee the white robe of scorn in which Herod clothed Jesus.

Eternal Father, I offer thee the column of the flagellation, the cords which bound Jesus, and the fearful instruments with which they tore his flesh.

Eternal Father, I offer thee the royal crown of thorns, the scarlet mantle, and the reed which he held in his Divine Hands.

Eternal Father, I offer thee the steps which Jesus mounted and watered with his precious Blood when Pilate showed him to the people, saying: "Behold the Man!"

Eternal Father, I offer thee the cords which bound Jesus as a criminal.

Eternal Father, I offer thee the sentence of death which was pronounced upon thy only Son.

Eternal Father, I offer thee the rods which were used to strike Jesus on the road to Calvary.

Eternal Father, I offer thee the Veil of St. Veronica upon which Jesus impressed his Divine Features.

Eternal Father, I offer thee the hammers used in the Crucifixion of Jesus.

Eternal Father, I offer thee the vase from which Jesus tasted the bitter draught.

Eternal Father, I offer thee the reed and sponge used to present Jesus the gall and vinegar.

Eternal Father, I offer thee the Holy Cross of Jesus, empurpled with his blood, and the inscription Pilate had attached to it: *"Jesus of Nazareth, King of the Jews!"*

Eternal Father, I offer thee the sacred vesture of Jesus, sanctified by his tears, sweat, and blood, and upon which the soldiers cast lots.

Eternal Father, I offer thee the sandals worn by the Sacred Feet of Jesus.

Eternal Father, I offer thee the garments of Jesus, covered with blood and divided in four parts by the soldiery.

Eternal Father, I offer thee the lance which opened the Sacred Side of Jesus and pierced his most loving Heart, making it our place of refuge.

Eternal Father, I offer thee all the instruments of torture used to accomplish the Passion of thy Divine Son Jesus.

Eternal Father, I offer thee the aromatics and perfumes which embalmed the Sacred Body of Jesus.

Eternal Father, I offer thee the holy winding-sheet and the bands which were honored in shrouding the Sacred Body of Jesus.

Eternal Father, I offer thee the holy sepulcher which enclosed the sacred corpse of Jesus, the divine source of life.

Eternal Father, I offer thee all the holy relics of thy Divine Jesus, humbly praying thee to look upon them with complacency. This divine look will render them more honor than can be rendered by all angels and saints. It will be a very worthy reparation for the profanations of which they have been the object.

Arrest, O Divine Father, the instruments of thy justice, *ready to strike us!* Behold the instruments of the most Sacred Passion of Jesus, red with his Adorable Blood. May this sight change thy justice to mercy and move thee to speak peace to France and the world.

Prayers.

I salute thee, Jesus of Nazareth. King of the Jews. Thou art the blessed Wheat of Nazareth, the delicious Bread of Bethlehem, the Lamb of God immolated at Jerusalem. Feed us poor sinners now and at the hour of our death. Amen.

We give thee glory, O most amiable Heart of Jesus, wounded by the impious of all ages. As a sword they have sharpened their tongues, and pierced thee by their injuries, blasphemies, and sarcasms. We invoke thee, and we celebrate thy praises in a spirit of honor and Reparation.

Eternal Father, I offer thee the most Holy Face of thy Divine Son to appease thy wrath. Remember his Divine Head has borne the thorns of our sins and has set itself to receive the strokes of thy justice, of which he still bears the marks. Behold these Holy Wounds! Incessantly they cry out to thee: Mercy, mercy, mercy for the whole world!

Eternal Father, I offer thee the Holy Face of Jesus for the spiritual needs of poor sinners. It is the golden coin which alone can cancel their debts.

A Little Exercise
IN HONOR OF THE FIVE WOUNDS.

Wound of the Right Hand.—Jesus, Son of Mary, who hast the power to forgive sins, grant me the remission of my faults through the merits of thy Holy Passion.

Wound of the Left Hand.—Jesus, Son of Mary, who art a God of union, grant me the grace to communicate worthily.

Wound of the Left Foot.—Jesus, who art the light of the world, deign to breathe in my soul the spirit of the Comforter.

Wound of the Right Foot.—Jesus, Son of Mary, who art Infinite Mercy, cleanse me in thy precious Blood.

Wound of the Sacred Heart.—Jesus, Son of Mary, who hast merited heaven for us, grant us eternal life.

Eternal Father, I offer thee the Five Wounds of thy Divine Son. We beseech thee to infuse in our souls the Divine Spirit which proceeds from thee and him; by the merits of the Sacred Passion of Jesus nourish our souls with the Living Bread of the Blessed Sacrament of the Altar.

Aspirations.

Sacred Body of Jesus, that I have received in the most Blessed Sacrament of the Altar, preserve my soul unto eternal life.

Jesus, Son of Mary, who hast been crowned with cruel thorns, grant that we may arrive at union with Thee.

Jesus, Son of Mary, who hast three times inclined thy Divine Face to the earth in the Garden of Olives, deign to incline towards the earth of my heart, and water it tears, thy sweat, and thy precious Blood.

Spirit of Love, Tongue of fire, impress upon my heart the thrice Holy Name of God.

Spirit of Consolation, by Holy Communion fill our souls with thy gifts and fruits.

I salute thee, O Mary. Spouse of the Holy Ghost, conjure him to come and dwell in us.

A Prayer for the Church

O God, by thy Holy Name have pity on us, protect us, and save us.

O good Jesus, in thy sweet Name guard our Sovereign Pontiff; breathe into his soul the spirit of the Comforter.

Jesus, thy Church is menaced with great trials! . . . Holy Father, by the virtue of thy salutary Name protect the Church of Jesus Christ. This was the last will of thy Divine Son; it is the holy prayer which love prompted towards the end of his life. *Holy Father, keep in thy Name those thou hast given me* (St. John chap, xxvii. 11).

O most holy and worthy Mother, refuge of the Church, intercede for us and save us by the Name of our Lord Jesus Christ.

St. Michael and the Holy Angels, guard the bark of Peter; disperse its enemies by the Holy Cross of our Lord Jesus Christ.

Devotions
IN HONOR OF THE HOLY INFANT JESUS.

The Month of the Divine Infant.

On the 15th of the month Sister Saint-Pierre celebrated the Espousals of the Blessed Virgin with St. Joseph. The 16th was consecrated to the mystery of the Incarnation. The nine following days she honored the Infant Jesus in the chaste womb of Mary, and accompanied the Blessed Virgin and St. Joseph in their journey to Bethlehem. On the 25th she celebrated the birth of the Holy Infant. On the 26th she adored him with the shepherds; on the 27th in his Circumcision when he was named Jesus; on the 28th with the three kings; on the 29th in his Presentation in the Temple; on the 30th in his Flight into Egypt.

The first seven days of the following month were consecrated to the Infant Jesus in his place of exile; she honored there his first words, steps, actions, his purity and simplicity. On the 8th she celebrated the return of the Holy Family to Nazareth.

On the 9th she contemplated Jesus beginning to work with St. Joseph.

On the 10th she honored the obedience of the Infant Jesus to his parents.

On the 11th she recalled the filial attentions he showed to his Blessed Mother and the faithful Guardian of his infancy. The 12th was consecrated to the journey of the Infant Jesus when at the age of twelve years he went with Mary and Joseph, to celebrate the Pasch, and also to the loss of the Child Jesus..

On the 13th she adored him in the midst of the Doctors of the Law, maintaining the rights of his Father. On the 14th she rendered homage to the Child found in the Temple by Mary and Joseph, and his returning in their company to Nazareth, where he was subject to them.

Admirabile Nomen Jesu, quod est super omne nomen. Venite, adoremus—"The Name which shall be called wonderful, the Name of Jesus, is the Name which is above every name. Oh! come, let us worship him."

(Sister Saint-Pierre was accustomed to repeat this beautiful invitatory thousands of times, and received signal graces there-by.)

Prayers
IN HONOR OF THE INFANT JESUS AND HIS BLESSED MOTHER.

An Act of Adoration to the Incarnate Word in the august Bosom of the Immaculate Virgin.

O Word Divine, incarnate for me, I adore thee, and I love thee with all my heart!

Eternal Wisdom, come and teach us the way to heaven!

O King of kings, come and reign over the hearts of all men, particularly over mine!

Come, all ye Angels, all ye men; come, all creatures, and unite with me in adoring a God so humbled!

O Holy Virgin, O Blessed St. Joseph, obtain for me such a great purity of heart that this Divine Infant may not be obliged to seek shelter in a stable on finding in my soul obstacles to his graces!

May my heart be ever open to him, may he make it his throne, and may all the powers of my soul be submissive to him!

Open, ye Heavens! O Mary, give us our King and our Saviour!

Prayer to the Infant Jesus.

O Divine Infant Jesus, by the love which impelled thee to take Flesh in the bosom of thy Holy Mother, and by that same love which made thee find means to give thyself to us, I pray thee most humbly to pardon all my sins, to destroy in me the old man and clothe me with thyself, so that I may no longer live but in thee and for thee, in honor of the abasement of thy Divinity, which was united to our humanity.

Offerings
IN HONOR OF THE DIVINE INFANT JESUS,

As *a preparation for the twenty-fifth of each month.*

First Offering.—Eternal Father, I offer to thy honor and glory, and for my own salvation and for the salvation of the whole world, the mystery of the Birth of our Divine Saviour.

Gloria Patri, etc.

Second Offering.—Eternal Father, I offer to thy honor and glory, and for my eternal salvation, the sufferings of the most Holy Virgin and St. Joseph in that long and weary journey from Nazareth to Bethlehem. I offer thee the sorrows of their hearts when they found no place wherein to shelter themselves when the Saviour of the world was to be born.

Gloria Patri, etc.

Third Offering.—*Eternal* Father, I offer to thy honor and glory, and for my eternal salvation, the sufferings of Jesus in the stable where he was born, the cold he endured, the swaddling-clothes which bound him, the tears he shed, and his tender infant cries.*Gloria Patri,* etc.

Fourth Offering.—Eternal Father, I offer to thy honor and glory, and for my eternal salvation, the pain which the Holy Child felt in his tender Body when he submitted to Circumcision. I offer thee that precious Blood which then, for the first time, he shed for the salvation of the whole human race.

Gloria Patri, etc.

Fifth Offering.—Eternal Father, I offer to thy honor and glory, and for my eternal salvation, the humility, mortification, patience, charity, all the virtues of the Child Jesus; and I thank thee, and I love thee, and I bless thee without end for the ineffable mystery of the Incarnation of the Divine Word.

Gloria Patri, etc.

V. The Word was made Flesh.

R. And dwelt amongst us.

Let us Pray.

O God, whose only-begotten Son was made manifest to us in the substance of our flesh, grant, we beseech thee, that through him, whom we acknowledge to be like unto ourselves, our souls may be inwardly renewed. Who liveth and reigneth with thee for ever and ever. Amen.

(An Indulgence of one year to all the faithful who, with contrite heart and devotion in public or in private, on any of the nine days preceding the twenty-fifth of the month, shall recite these five Offerings with the versicle and prayer.)

Gospel of the Holy Name of Jesus

There is no other name under Heaven given to men whereby we must be saved. *(Acts* iv. 12.)

In the name of Jesus let every knee bow, of things in Heaven, of things on earth, and of things under the earth, and let every tongue confess that our Lord Jesus Christ is in the glory of God the Father. *(Phil.* ii. 10.)

Explanations of the Devotion to the Little Gospel of the Holy Name of Jesus.

Our Lord himself teaches us to invoke his Holy Name: "Whatsoever you shall ask the Father in my name shall be given to you." St. Paul says: "Whosoever shall call on the name of the Lord shall be saved." The victory gained over the demon by our Lord, and expressed by his Name of Jesus, which means Saviour, being a grace drawn from his Sacred Heart, its image is affixed to the little sachet containing the Gospel of the Holy Name of Jesus, as a seal is applied to a reliquary to guarantee the authenticity of the relic. In honor of the five letters of the Name of Jesus, and through the virtue of his Five Wounds, our Lord has promised to grant five special graces to those who embrace this devotion with faith and piety.

1. He will preserve them from lightning.

2. From the snares and malice of the demon.

3. From a sudden and unprovided death.

4. He will make them walk with facility in the way of virtue.-

5. He will grant them final perseverance.

Our Lord is pleased to manifest the power of his Holy Name by many other spiritual and temporal favors, such as conversions, cures, etc. This little sachet is particularly efficacious with dying sinners. The devotion to the Holy Name of Jesus is connected with that of the Reparation for Blasphemy by the *cultus* of the Holy Face.

(Extract from the Life of Sister Saint-Pierre, Carmelite of Tours, France, written by herself, and published with the approbation of the Archbishops of Tours and New Orleans.)

With the approbation of the Most Rev. Archbishop Gibbons.

This Gospel, and all else connected with the Confraternity of the Holy Face, can be found at 134 Barrack Street, New Orleans, La.

Jesus, be to me a Jesus!

Prayers to excite Confidence in the Invocation of the Adorable Name of Jesus.

"And after eight days were accomplished, that the Child should be circumcised, his name was called Jesus, which was called by the angel before lie was conceived in the womb." (Gospel of the Feast of the Circumcision: *Luke* ch. ii. v. 21.)

"For there is no other name under Heaven given to men whereby we must be saved." (Acts *of the Apostles* ch. iv. v. 12.)

Divine Saviour! through the victory thou hast gained over Satan by taking the Name of Jesus, deliver us from his snares.

Jesus, Son of God! have mercy on us!

Jesus, Son of the Virgin Mary! have mercy on us!

O Jesus and Mary! be propitious to us!

Make us, O Lord! to have a continual fear and love of thy Holy Name, because thou, dost never abandon the care of those who, by thy grace, cease not to love thee; who livest and reignest, one God, world without end. Amen.

Examined and approved.

Gentry, *Vic.-Gen.*

Tours, July 24, 1848.

When Jesus was named,

Satan, conquered, was disarmed.

An indulgence of twenty-five days for invoking the Holy Name of Jesus and Mary; fifty days' indulgence to those who wear the Blue

Scapular, plenary indulgence at the hour of death; twenty days for reverently bowing the head when pronouncing these sacred names; an indulgence of fifty days as often as two persons salute each other, the one saying, in any language whatever, "Praised be Jesus and Mary"; and the other replying, "Now and forever." (Pius IX, Sept. 26, 1864.)

Prayer to the Holy Name.

May the Adorable Name of Jesus be the sweet and daily music of my soul and the joy of my heart; and when, in the agony and cold sweat of death, I give the last look for mercy, may the parting sigh of my soul be, Jesus! Jesus! Amen.

Prayers
IN HONOR OF THE MATERNITY OF THE BLESSED VIRGIN MARY.

O most holy and worthy Mother of God, impart abundantly to all mankind, thy children, the milk of grace and mercy.

Hail, Mary, conceived without sin, mysterious vine which has produced the Divine Grape, destined to be crushed in the wine-press of the Cross, whence issued a sacred wine that was deposited in the precious vase of thy Immaculate Heart, to be distilled upon the children whose Mother thou didst become upon Calvary's mount.

O Divine Infant Jesus, I adore thee on thy Blessed Mother's bosom. Yes, O Divine Infant, in this state of humiliation and littleness thou art as worthy of our love, our homage, and adoration as when thou didst cure the sick, raise the dead to life, and command the winds and waves.

Here do I contemplate thee, silent and unknown, adoring thy Eternal Father's counsels upon thy life and dolorous Passion. Already is the Cross planted in thy Heart; thou dost only await the hour marked by thy Heavenly Father for thee to fulfil his will.

Hail, Queen of Martyrs! whose precious blood, blanched by maternal piety, flowed for fifteen months from thy virginal bosom to fill the sacred veins of the King of Martyrs.

O holy Virgin, how pure and admirable thou art! The Holy Ghost seems ever occupied with thee. At thy birth I hear him saying in his Divine Council: "Our *Sister is little. . . . What shall we do with our Sister in the day when she is to be spoken to?*"

O mystery ineffable! He who eternally reposes in the Bosom of the Father rests at the same time in the bosom of an humble Virgin. I adore thee, most Holy Infant Jesus, in that royal shrine surrounded by roses and lilies; my soul experiences joy inexpressible at beholding thee dwelling in that *House of Gold* built by Supreme Wisdom.

Come forth, O Divine Jesus, from the virginal prison where love holds thee captive; give me the consolation of beholding and adoring thee, and in a state that I may embrace thee. Let us rejoice; the day of joy hath come at last, and the angels sing in heavenly strains, "Glory be to God on high, and on earth peace to men of good will!" The hour of man's salvation has dawned. Behold his Saviour, born of Mary. O earth, thou didst become a heaven on that day eternally memorable. O glorious Mother of God, my hopes are realized, my yearning satisfied, now that I find Jesus, my Redeemer, in thy holy arms, resting upon thy maternal bosom, nourished with thy virginal milk. I hear the heavenly Spouse felicitating thee on thy blessed maternity. Yes, thou art beautiful in the eyes of thy Spouse, because thou hast preserved intact the beautiful flower of virginity. While angels in heaven sing the eternal canticle of the thrice Holy God, we on earth sing the virginal canticle of the Mother thrice a virgin. O grandeur of Mary! O incomparable privilege! O mystery of love!

Hail Mary, full of grace, the Lord is with thee; blessed art thou amongst women, and blessed is the Fruit of thy womb, Jesus, whom thou didst nourish during fifteen months with thy virginal milk.

We give thee thanks, O Blessed Virgin Mary, for the great love with which thou didst suckle the King of Heaven, and we bless thy maternal tenderness.

Eternal Father, we offer thee the Incarnate Word, a Babe at his Blessed Mother's breast, rendering thee by this lowly action perfect praise for the honor and glory of thy Holy Name.

O most holy and sweet Mother of God, remember thou art my Mother and that I am the little sister of the Holy Infant Jesus.

Thy Divine Son has left upon thy bosom the charming virtues of his Holy Infancy, and he sends me to gather this celestial dew, which will fill my soul with purity, innocence, and simplicity.

Receive, O Virgin and Mother, these fifteen salutations in memory of the fifteen months during which thou didst nurse the Lamb of God, born in the stable of Bethlehem.

O holy and august Mother, what dost thou do? "I give my milk to him who hath given me being." And what will become of this milk? "It will become his Flesh and the Blood of his veins. This Flesh which I give him will suffer the torments of his Passion, and this Blood obtained from me will be shed upon the Cross for the salvation of sinners."

O Angels of Heaven, what think ye of this prodigy? It was once your mission to give man delicious food on earth by showering manna from Heaven, and this was truly a great miracle. But behold now, with admiration inexpressible, the Virgin Mother, your Queen, nourishing God himself, her Creator and yours.

O Divine Blood of Jesus, refresh the earth that it may bring forth elect souls.

(Our Lord promised that all who would thus honor him should receive great blessings, that they would be especially assisted by his Blessed Mother, and that he would grant all their petitions. Holy Church keeps the Feast of the Maternity of the Blessed Virgin on the second Sunday in October.)

Sister Saint-Pierre's Prayer
TO THE QUEEN OF CARMEL FOR THE HOUSES OF HER ORDER.

"O Holy Mary, sprinkle the flowers of Carmel with thy fruitful grace, that they may thus become so strongly rooted in this land of benediction as never to be eradicated by the demon."

The *O Gloriosa Virginum* seventy-two times in honor of her Divine Maternity.

Come, Jesus, come! *Sit Nomen Domini benedictum.*

Mother most pure, pray for us. O Mary, Mother of God, source of all our joy for time and eternity, be thou our strength. Lead us to the arms of thy Divine Child and teach us his winning ways. When earth and sense shall fail show us thy gentle face, and in thy pure embrace let us meet the merciful gaze of our Saviour Jesus. Amen.

Our Lady of La Salette

On the 19th of September, 1846, Our Blessed Lady appeared upon an Alpine mountain called La Salette to humble little shepherds named Maximin and Melanie, two innocent children through whose mouths she reproached "her people" of France for their blasphemy and impiety. Tears were flowing from her eyes; the crucifix was fixed upon her heart. She was surrounded by the instruments of the Passion, and the cruel hammer and sharp pincers were the ornaments of her maternal bosom.

Novena to Our Lady of La Salette.

O my Blessed Lady Queen of Heaven, to thee and to thy sacred keeping, into the bosom of thy mercy, this day and every day until the hour of my death, I commend my body and soul; my every hope, joy, and sorrow, my life and the end of my life, I commend to thee, that every act may be according to thy will and that of thy Divine Son. Amen.

Nine "Hail Marys," with the following Aspiration after each:

Our Lady of La Salette, refuge of sinners, our reconciler with God, pray without ceasing for your children who have recourse to thee. Amen.

Our Lady of La Salette, pray for us. Amen.

Exercise in Honor of Our Lady of La Salette.

1. I salute thee, blessed soul of Mary, image of the Divinity. *Ave Maria!*

2. I revere thee, sacred body of Mary, living temple of the Holy Spirit. *Ave Maria!*

3. I bless thee, precious blood of Mary, from which was formed the Body of the Man-God. *Ave Maria!*

4. I kiss with profound respect the charitable feet of Mary, which did not disdain to descend upon the mountain of La Salette for the salvation of France. *Ave Maria!*

5. I exalt thee, most pure hands of Mary, who for the first time offered to the Eternal Father the Host without stain. *Ave Maria!*

6. I venerate thee, chaste bosom of Mary, as the sanctuary of God, sacred ostensorium of the Incarnate Word. *Ave Maria!*

7. I invoke thee, Immaculate Heart of Mary, ardent furnace of charity. *Ave Maria!*

8. I solicit thee, blessed ears of Mary, always attentive and propitious to the cries of the unfortunate. *Ave Maria!*

9. I admire thee, beautiful eyes of Mary, full of sweetness and compassion, always open to our needs and ready to supply them. May we experience the virtue of thy charitable gaze. *Ave Maria!*

10. I regard thee with love, incomparable mouth of Mary, which pleads our cause without ceasing before the Sovereign Judge, and continually obtains favorable judgment. *Ave Maria!*

11. I contemplate thee with joy, resplendent face of Mary, radiant with beauty and glory. Give to thy children the kiss of maternal love as a pledge of the treaty of peace, which we pray thee to obtain from a God irritated on account of our crimes. *Ave Maria!*

12. I salute thee, rainbow of mercy in the day of storm; appear before our terrified eyes and prevent the thunderbolt striking our guilty heads. *Ave Maria! Memorare.*

Our Lady of the Holy Name of God, may thou be blessed in all times and all places.

(For connection between the *cultus* of the Holy Face and La Salette, see *Life of Sister Saint-Pierre*)

Forty Days' Prayer
FOR THE NEEDS OF THE CHURCH ANDSTATE.

Commenced by M. Dupont in 1843.

May God arise and his enemies be dispersed! Say three *Pater Nosters,* three *Ave Marias,* and three *Gloria Patris.*

St. Michael and all the holy Angels, pray and combat for us.

St. Peter and all the holy Apostles, intercede for us.

St. Ignatius, St. Teresa, and all the inhabitants of the Heavenly Jerusalem, pray for us.

Aspiration during the Day.

May thy Holy Name, O Lord, be known and blessed in all times and places.

Blessed Virgin Mary, reign over us with thy Divine Son Jesus. Amen.

(This devotion is made from July 16, Feast of Our Lady of Mt. Carmel, until August 25, Feast of St. Louis, King and Protector of France.)

Salutation
TO THE HOLY VEIL OF ST. VERONICA

The greater Relic of the Vatican Basilica.

Antiphon.

My heart speaks to thee; my eyes seek thee; yes, Lord, I will always seek thy Face. Do not hide thy Face from me; do not turn away from thy servant.

V. O Lord, thou hast shown to me the light of thy Face.

R. Thou hast given joy to my heart.

Let us Pray.

Grant in thy mercy, O Lord, that my soul, created by thy wisdom and governed by thy providence, may be filled with the light of thy Holy Face, through our Lord Jesus Christ. Amen.

Canticles
IN HONOR OF THE HOLY FACE.

From the French of Sister Saint-Pierre
BY M. E. HENRY.

Canticle First.

i.

From out the sanctuary's silence
What sighs are those I hear?
What bitter cry is breaking
From thy soul, O Saviour dear?
"Alas! the whole world wounds me
With blasphemy's swift dart;
My love hath lost its power
O'er man's forgetful heart.

ii.

"With deadly hatred banded,
Schism walks forth today,
The holiest laws defying,
Impatient of their sway;
And my Face, that highest rapture
In the vision of the blest,
With a constant memory cruel
Of their outrage is impressed.

iii.

"O ye to whose brave spirits
My glory is so near,
To whom my victory cometh.
My triumph is so dear,
Ye are my cherished spouses;
My name e'er holy keep,
Asking ever for the guilty
Pardon and sorrow deep.

iv.

"Of old, before my Passion,
Veronica, with love's great power.
Clad with courage, seemed to soften
All the anguish of that hour.
Another Veronica I now long for
Who, adoring night and day,
On my bleeding brow unceasing
The veil of her true love shall lay.

v.

"And Veronica, the faithful,
My grateful memory knew;
Of my Holy Face forever
She kept the Image true.
To ye also I now leave it;
Let your hearts be impressed deep,
And with love's tender homage
A fervent incense keep.

vi.

"In this Countenance divine
The Godhead is concealed;
'Tis the mirror where his beauty

Eternal is revealed.

Ah! Christian soul, if only

Thou knewest the holy spell

Of that Face, what supreme rapture

Would in thy spirit swell!

vii.

"On the Brow behold the Father,

From the lips list to the Son,

In the eyes' pure light the Spirit

Of the Holy Three-in-One.

And these sacred tresses, countless,

The symbols seem to be

Of the attributes surrounding

The God-like Trinity.

viii.

"This Holy Face reflecting

My Blest Humanity

Is for thee the precious ransom

Paid for thine eternity.

None have ever met denial

Who looked to its priceless worth,

That Face of treasures holiest

That await the elect of earth.

ix.

"Alas! blasphemy's outrage

Wounds me on every side;

Have I no brave defenders

In whom I may confide?

Avenge me, faithful virgins.

My cruel wrongs repair;

Be yours the gentle vengeance

Of love and tears and prayer.

x.

"Within your hearts my Image

Deeply shall ye enshrine,

Till its beauty shall enkindle

The fires of love divine.

And this Face for e'er adored

The sign and the seal shall be

Of the grace which shall be thy greeting In a blest eternity."

Canticle Second.

Lord Jesus, our God, our Brother,

We have grieved thee,

O Saviour above;

Before thy Face, God-like and lonely,

We pour out our tears and our love.

Refrain: Face ever adored,

Behold 'neath thee now

A people most sinful

In penitence bow.

ii.

See the Brow, where the thorns are piercing,

And the Face—ah! God, is it thine?

The tears and the blood of Redemption

Are veiling those Eyes divine.

Face ever adored, etc.

iii.

"We have seen him," crieth the prophet,

"Without beauty, deserted, alone,

As a reed all bruised by the tempest,

As a leper cast forth from his own."

Face ever adored, etc.

iv.

Of the sons of men the fairest,

Bright Mirror of splendors divine.

Behold him, for thou art, O sinner.

His tormentor; the lashes are thine.

Face ever adored, etc.

v.

Holy Face, on that night most cruel

Thou with infamous blows wast stained;

The Most High, the God thrice holy,

By the fury of wretches profaned.

Face ever adored, etc.

vi.

We were there; our hands have wounded

Our Christ. Ah! sinners, 'tis true;

We were the faithless companions,

False friends—we deserted him, too.

Face ever adored, etc.

vii.

Forgive us, O Jesus, our Victim!

Forgive them that slight thee, we pray;

When before thee we kneel in sorrow,

Thy Face, Lord, turn not away.

Face ever adored, etc.

viii.

Holy Face, our days and our vigils,
Our vows and our tears, are thine;
The world seeks its false pleasures,
We are shielding the Face divine.
Face ever adored, etc.

ix.

We shield thee, and thou wilt shield us—
Thy sorrows to us belong;
Our brows are pure when thou lookest,
And near thee our hearts are strong.
Face ever adored, etc.

x.

Face Divine, Face ever desired,
Our steps turn ceaseless to thee;
Face of God, for ever adored,
Where thou waitest us soon let us be.
Face ever adored, etc.

Canticle to St. Peter Repenting.

i.

Before the Altar, where the soul repentant.
Beholding God, with sin and sorrow crushed,
Remembers and adores Love immolated,
The heart dejected, powerless, is hushed.
First Refrain: Oh! holy tears,
Heart-voices flow,
Telling its fears,
Regrets, and woe.

ii.

Ah! fruitful tears, how oft our souls have sought ye,
How oft we waited for ye, all in vain;
Bring forth from their deep sources, O mighty Patron,
Of love repentant bring our tears, blest rain.
Oh! holy tears, etc.

iii.

Thrice in that night of blasphemy had
Peter Faltered, and, alas! his Lord denied.
Ah! sinners, let us weep—weep for ourselves
And for the countless sins we cannot hide;
Oh! holy tears, etc.

iv.

When Peter saw its look on him as a sinner,
He was the first conquest of the Holy Face;
Already wounded but divine for ever,
It blest and pardoned him with mercy's grace.
Oh! holy tears, etc.

v.

And when his Lord had once looked on Peter
Grief smote him, and, with swift, repentant cry.
He wept for his sin; and those dews penitential
Dwelt ever in his eyes till life's last sigh.
Oh! holy tears, etc.

vi.

But one blest day the stream that o'er his spirit
In sorrow flowed a sweeter measure traced;
The triple sin was blotted out for ever—
Was by the triple oath of love effaced.
Oh! holy tears, etc.

Second Refrain: Oh! sweet tears, flow;

Come, fervor true,

Your power show,

And our hearts subdue.

vii.

"Thou knowest, Lord, I love thee," vows the Apostle,

And from Christ's feet arises, all the weight

The supreme burden bearing of Chief Shepherd;

His tears of love crown him and consecrate!

Oh! sweet tears, flow, etc.

viii.

Thou who thyself didst know one human weakness,

Thou who thy God's forgiveness sweet didst taste.

Thou whom he vested with his wondrous powers

To open for us Heaven's riches, haste!

Oh! sweet tears, flow, etc.

ix.

The Church, alas! like Christ at the Tribunal,

Ever on dread Calvary's Mount appears.

Around our Mother's feet, then, let us sorrow;

But let Hope strengthen, make sweet our tears.

Oh ! sweet tears, flow, etc.

x.

For we have loved her, holy Church immortal,

Where thou dost live again, the Three-in-One.

She keeps thy faith; help us, O God! to give her

Our tears and blood, even as thou hast done.

Oh! sweet tears, flow, etc.

A Rhythm

(Pope John XII, elected Sovereign Pontiff at Avignon in 1316, wrote the following prayer in honor of the Most Holy Veil, and granted an Indulgence of twenty-five years and twenty-five quarantines to the faithful who would recite it. To those who cannot read the same Indulgence is granted provided five Our Fathers, five Hail Marys, and the Gloria be said for the same intention.)

I.

Hail, token of love to Veronica given!
Stamped divinely on linen, without spot or stain,
Pure and bright with the splendor that comes but from Heaven;
O features most sacred of Jesus, all hail!

ii.

Hail, glory of earth, of thy faithful the Mirror!
'Tis to see thy blest Face Thrones and Virtues aspire!
Send afar from us all the dark stains of error,
That with thee at last we may find our desire.

iii.

Hail, features most sacred! hail, Face of my Saviour!
Oh! shed on us here the sweet light of thy love.
From on High thou receiv'dst the Omnipotent favor
Of freeing our senses from all but thy love.

iv.

Hail, rampart of Faith! be with us for ever;
Before thee dread Heresy's poisonous dart
Is dispelled. Bless thy people; oh! let us ne'er sever
Our eyes from thy features, our love from thy Heart.

v.

Hail, refuge in sorrow, and help in our way!
Through this lifetime of danger oh! be our tried friend;
Call us ever, blessed Image, to Heaven away,
Where thy radiant Face beckons us to ascend.

vi.

Hail, Jesus Divine! hail, diamond most bright!
O'er the light of the firmament shines thy soft ray.
God himself formed these lines, beauteous, fair in *his* sight,
And without mortal aid bid these blest Features to stay.

vii.

Hail, reflection unchanging, of joy without end!
The glory Divine which on thee appears
Is ever as pure as when first to us given;
O Beauty e'er new, thou fad'st not in years.

viii.

Hail, Essence of Majesty, Sacred yet kind!
Thy Face the calm impress of purity bears;
Oh! let us not *Justice* but sweet *Piercy* find,
And grant us in Heaven a rest from our fears I

ix.

Oh! be our loved Refuge, our Help, and our Star;
Be a soft, soothing balm to our hearts, till above,
In the calm rest eternal of thy Heaven afar,
We may praise thee for ever and ever in love.

Amen.

Let us Pray.

Give joy to the countenance of thy servants, O my Lord, and save
our souls from the darkness of hell, that, being protected by the
contemplation of thy Adorable Face, we may trample on all carnal
desires, and see thee, O Lord Jesus, our Saviour, face to face, without

fear, when the clouds of Heaven will open to admit us to thy
judgment. Amen.

A Rhythm

(The following prayer was composed by Pope Clement VI at Avignon.
His Holiness granted an indulgence of three years to all those who
would recite it before a *Vera Effigies,* or authentic fac-simile of the Veil
of St. Veronica.)

i.

O venerated Features, hail!
On the bleeding altar of the Cross,
Alas! how altered and how pale!
Thou look'st so sorrowful and sad,
Staining with thy Sweat and Blood
This precious Veil and wood!

ii.

Token of thy Passion sad,
This Veil is brightest even now;
'Twas stamped and given for our Redemption.
Inflame my soul, sweet Jesus, teach
My heart the fire of thy love;
Reveal to us thy Features fair above.

iii.

Oh! grant me, at the end of life,
Of God the beauty for ever to see;
Give to my then transported soul
The bliss of Heaven's felicity. Amen.

V. Make the light of thy Countenance, O Lord, to shine upon us,
R. Thou hast given gladness to my heart.

V. Save thy servant.

R. Trusting in thee, O my God.

V. Save me in thy mercy, O Lord.

R. Let me not be confounded, for I have called upon thy Name.

V. Make thy Face to shine upon thy servant.

R. And teach me thy way upon earth.

V. O Lord God of Hosts, convert us.

R. And show thy Face, and we shall be saved.

V. O Lord, hear my prayer.

R. And let my cry come unto thee.

Let us Pray.

O God, who hast shed upon us the light of thy Face, and who wast pleased, through Veronica, to leave us thy Holy Image imprinted on this veil as an eternal token of thy love, grant us by thy Passion and Cross the grace so to honor, adore and glorify thee here below, through this mystical Veil, that we may without fear meet thy gaze when thou wilt receive and us in Heaven. Amen.

O Eternal and Omnipotent God, whose Divine Features are revealed through this precious Image to thy people here assembled, grant us the pardon of our sins, and direct our actions, words, senses, and faculties. We trust in thy mercy, O Lord, who liveth and reigneth with thee in the unity of the Holy Ghost, one God, world without end. Amen.

Devout Address to the Sacred Face

O Face Divine!

O Face most sorrowful yet so benign!

So beauteous still in grief, towards me incline!

O Sacred Eyes!

On which the weight of dreaded anguish lies,

That look must break the heart which Christ denies.

O Lips so meek!

Unless their all-absolving word I seek,

Those lips one day eternal doom will speak.

O Sacred Face!

Which mortal hand has dared with prayer to trace,

Thee on my heart with throbs of awe I place.

O Face Divine!

Give me of love returned some blissful sign;

O Face Divine, in grief towards me incline.